Books by Elizabeth Engstrom

Novels
When Darkness Loves Us
Black Ambrosia
Lizzie Borden
Lizard Wine
Black Leather
Candyland
The Northwoods Chronicles
York's Moon
Baggage Check
Guys Named Bob

Collections of Short Fiction
Nightmare Flower
The Alchemy of Love
Suspicions

Nonfiction Books
Something Happened to Grandma
How to Write a Sizzling Sex Scene
Divorce by Grand Canyon

Anthologies Edited
Word by Word (co-editor)
Imagination Fully Dilated (co-editor)
Imagination Fully Dilated vol. II (editor)
Dead on Demand (editor)
Pronto! Writings from Rome (co-editor)
Ship's Log: Writings at Sea (co-editor)
Lies and Limericks (co-editor)
Mota 9: Addiction (editor)

Praise for Elizabeth Engstrom

About *The Northwoods Chronicles*:

"*The Northwoods Chronicles* conjured up in me the same excitement and wonder I felt when I read Ray Bradbury's *The Martian Chronicles*. I was taken far away...inside my own heart, my fears, my hopes. I set it down to tend to life; forgot where I put it; got anxious just like Recon John when the monkey jawbone went missing. I finished it, but it's not over: I've been gifted with a life in a strange new world, not without its shadows, and the glimmer of weird on the water. This one is a keeper, and I'm one of its kept. Brava, Elizabeth Engstrom."
—Nancy Holder, author of *Son of the Shadows*

"To read Elizabeth Engstrom is to be guided by the sure hand of an accomplished writer whose stories have the power to transfer readers to places both real and surreal. We believe in the unbelievable, marvel at worlds created between dream and reality, and reach for all that transcends the limits of our imagination."
—Gail Tsukiyama, author of *The Street of a Thousand Blossoms*

"From the ominous opening to the soaring conclusion, these braided stories—subtle and spooky and smart—will keep the reader spellbound.. The Northwoods is a scary place to live, but in Ms. Engstom's hands, it's a fabulous visit."
—Karen Joy Fowler, author of *The Jane Austen Book Club*

"Were he still alive, Rod Serling would like Engstrom's book. Presented separately, each of her narratives would make a great segment of the classic "Twilight Zone" television program so popular in the 1960s. Taken together—and given Serling's absence among us—they give us another way to hold a book in our hands that gives our spines a tingle and makes us wonder if Serling is really so far away after all."
—*Eugene Register Guard*

About *Baggage Check*:

"The author is so deft at creating interesting, 3D characters that I was instantly hooked into Sweetann's plight (yes, Sweetann). Even the bad guys have depth and lives beyond the story. This is not a typical thriller which makes it much more interesting than the average shoot 'em up, and Sweetann is not a typical heroine. A guaranteed fun time."
—*Christina Lay, author of* Death is a Star, editor at Shadow Spinners Books

About *Black Leather*:

...a darkly seductive page-turner by a writer who knows how to put the erotic thrill into a thriller.
—*DarkEcho*

...an artfully written and highly recommended erotic and psychological suspense from first page to last.
—*Midwest Book Review*

About *Suspicions*:

"This is where she's at her best."
—*Locus*

"A spooky collection of tales."
—*Publishers Weekly*

"A hefty, genre-crossing pie spiced with images capable of snagging the imagination."
—*Booklist*

"Elizabeth Engstrom has selected twenty-five (four original to the collection) stories from the past twenty years of writing that reveal her as a suspicious sort. But then, aren't we all? We all suspect the unknown, death, sex, and "friends, family, love, work, technology, the government, and everything else." It's just that Elizabeth Engstrom can take her lack of trust and craft fine fiction from it. Like many fine writers, Engstrom's stories are across all genres. Some can be termed sf, others as mystery or fantasy or horror, still others are simply "fiction." A few are light and humorous. Most are quietly dark, slightly skewed, angled toward that indescribable place just at the edge of shadow. All are worth reading. Many are worth pondering. By the end, at least one suspicion will definitely be confirmed: Elizabeth Engstrom is one of the best. No doubts."

—*Cemetery Dance*

About *York's Moon*:

"*York's Moon* is so absorbing and unusual that you'll almost miss how beautifully written it is—almost. Elizabeth Engstrom's mesmerizing and unique style will draw you into a world of mystery, violence and heroic struggle. Ultimately, this story celebrates the uplifting power of the human spirit. Do not miss it."

—Susan Wiggs, bestselling author of *Marrying Daisy Bellamy*

"With quirky, engaging characters, *York's Moon* is as much about understanding the human condition as solving a murder mystery. I cannot imagine anyone but Liz Engstrom writing this fine novel."

—Terry Brooks, author of the *Shannara* series

About *Lizzie Borden*:

"Marvelous stuff. The pressures on Lizzie were vivid and completely real. You know, I think I'd have killed him myself..."

—Mercedes Lackey, author of the *Heralds of Valdemar* series

"Every door in the Borden house is metaphorically locked, and each room holds the terrible secrets of the occupant... Engstrom [moves] the reader inexorably toward the anticipated savage denouement."
—*Publishers Weekly*

"Elizabeth Engstrom has woven a fascinating tale of a lonely, tormented and frustrated young woman."
—*Rocky Mountain News*

About *Lizard Wine*:

"*Lizard Wine* is the book your mother warned you about, sleek, nasty, perfectly focused, smart as hell, absolutely convincing, and utterly single-minded. This novel wants to buy you a drink, whisper in your ear, coax you into a dark room and there seriously mess you up. Because Elizabeth Engtrom is a magnificently talented writer, her novel not only actually does these things, it leaves you grateful for the experience. *Lizard Wine* is the kind of book which enlarges and enriches the genre of the thriller."
—Peter Straub, author of *Ghost Story*

"...*Lizard Wine* is a book that will make your skin crawl."
—John Saul, author of *The Blackstone Chronicles*

"...hard! Should carry a health warning: Just reading this could leave you bruised..."
—Brian Lumley, author of the *Necroscope* series

"Excruciating suspense!"
—Bryce Courtenay, author of *The Power of One*

"*Lizard Wine* is a disturbing vintage... With a true literary voice, Elizabeth Engstrom details the madness of human

relationships... It is as if Franz Kafka, Tom Robbins and Shirley Jackson collaborated on a story which only Engstrom could write. A brilliant, page-turning read."
—Douglas Clegg, author of *The Children's Hour*

"Supertaut storytelling..."
—*Kirkus Reviews*

"I often stopped with a low mental whistle of awe at Engstrom's seamless style..."
—*DarkEcho*

"...Deliverance meets Misery..."
—*The Fiction Addiction*

"...Don't read this book alone at night."
—*Eugene Register Guard*

"...The message of *Lizard Wine* is clear. This could be anybody. This could be you."
—*AmericaOnline*

About *When Darkness Loves Us*:

"Finding the light when swamped in darkness is never an easy thing. *When Darkness Loves Us* is a collection of two novellas from Elizabeth Engstrom. One story follows a young farm girl as she is engulfed by an underworld and yearns to escape, and an old woman who is facing the monsters of her past. Two engaging stories make *When Darkness Loves Us* quite a pick."
—*Midwest Book Review*

"Fresh, inventive, stylish and captivating."
—Dean Koontz

"A moving story of redemption and love."
—*West Coast Review of Books*

"A masterpiece, and one of the finest tragedies I've read in years."
—*Horror Show*

"Behind that soft-voiced style is power, is surprise, is... ferocity."
—Theodore Sturgeon

Divorce by Grand Canyon

8 Riveting True Crime stories

by Elizabeth Engstrom

IFD Publishing

P.O. Box 40776, Eugene, Oregon 97404 U.S.A.
www.ifdpublishing.com

Divorce by Grand Canyon
Copyright © 2019 by Elizabeth Engstrom

All rights reserved. No part of this book may be reproduced or transmitted in any form or by any means, electronic or mechanical, including photocopying, recording, or by any information storage and retrieval system, without the written consent of the publisher, except where permitted by law.

Cover art, Copyright © 2019 Alan M. Clark

ISBN: 978-0-9996656-9-5

Printed in the United States of America

Divorce by Grand Canyon

8 Riveting True Crime stories

by Elizabeth Engstrom

Eugene, Oregon

Divorce by Grand Canyon

Introduction — 15

Trials of Christian Longo — 16

The Majesty of Maggots — 35

Jeremy Bryan Jones: Meth Monster — 45

Joel Patrick Courtney: A Horrifying Progression of Sex Offenses — 62

Patrick Wayne Kearney and David Douglas Hill: The Trash Bag Murderers — 75

Russell Obremski: A Killer's Luck — 90

Robert Spangler: Divorce by Grand Canyon — 107

Gabriel Morris: Mormon, Missionary, Murderer — 124

About the Author — 173

Introduction

It has been said that if being a writer doesn't turn you into a professional psychologist, it will certainly turn you into an amateur one. Delving deeply into fictional characters' minds and motivations requires a depth of study into the human condition.

In my mind, nothing is more interesting than the twisted motivations of those who behave outside the norm of society. My interest isn't clinical; I am interested in finding out how they justify their actions. We all justify the things we do, even if they're not in our own best interests. The people in this book all have unique and sometimes elaborate justifications for their actions.

If there's anything I've learned over the years, it's this: Scratch the surface and you'll find a story. These stories are, to me, extraordinary, but we all have our stories, and they're all interesting ones.

The first seven stories were originally written for Court TV's Crime Library. The last story was originally published as "Something Happened to Grandma" by Rosetta Books.

—Elizabeth Engstrom
Eugene, Oregon

The Trials of Christian Longo

Two Tragic Deaths

On December 19, 2001, a young boy's body floated up in Lint Slough, not far from the coastal town of Newport, Oregon. He seemed to be about four years old and wore only his underpants. Three days later, divers found the body of a slightly younger little girl, still in nine feet of murky water, under the Lint Slough Bridge, still tethered to the bottom by a pillowcase full of rocks tied around her ankle. Divers found a similar weighted pillowcase, which had apparently been tied around the boy's ankle. Also, in those waters was a sleeping bag full of rocks. Authorities never released a cause of death for the two children, other than it was not due to trauma. Speculation has it that the two children were weighted down by their own cartoon pillowcases full of rocks, both shoved into the sleeping bag and thrown off the bridge into the slough—while still alive.

Thus, began the largest crime investigation in the history of Lincoln County, Oregon.

The Boy, the Family, the Religion

It's hard to say when Christian Longo learned the art of standing politely, passively, while smooth-talking his way out of trouble. This calmness served him well from the time his financial troubles began by stealing a roll of quarters from his father's dresser when in ninth grade—all the way to the

Attribution: Ninian Reid from Perth, Scotland
Photo title: An eye for an eye, a tooth for a tooth: Family killer Christian Longo is sentenced to death in an Oregon courtroom
Alterations: converted to grayscale.

day twenty Mexican police and FBI agents crashed into his Caribbean hideaway and arrested him for the murder of his wife and three children. Had he been the aggressive sort—resisting arrest, showing his temper when faced with the evidence of his crimes—things may have turned out much differently for Christian and his family. As it was, he passively submitted to handcuffs as his horrified German girlfriend looked on. He was not the *New York Times* journalist Michael Finkel after all. Instead, she was informed, he was Christian Longo, one of the FBI's Ten Most Wanted, and he was headed for death row.

Longo's crimes began as a simple, perhaps even logical way out of his financial woes, and escalated into one of the most heinous crimes to have captured the imagination of the country. Longo's crimes, pursuit, capture and trial made headlines coast to coast, were highlighted on "America's Most Wanted" television show, and the subject of Michael Finkel's book, *True Story: Murder, Memoir, Mea Culpa.*

Born in Burlington, Iowa, Christian and his younger brother moved several times around the Midwest with their mother and father, following employment opportunities. Eventually, that marriage crumbled, and Joy, the mother, remarried and settled in Ann Arbor, Michigan when the boys were still small. The entire family embraced the Jehovah's Witness religion of Joe Longo, the boys' stepfather. The small Jehovah's Witness community in Ypsilanti seemed an oasis for the Longos—it provided a code of ethics, a community in which to socialize and marry—a manner of behavior that was a refreshing dose of sanity to the reconstituted family with a harsh past. It was within this insular religious community that Christian, at seventeen, met MaryJane Baker, seven years his senior. Deemed by his parents still too young to date girls at age eighteen, Christian got a job at a local camera store and moved out of the house to pursue the beautiful MaryJane.

The Love Story

MaryJane Baker, a sweet, unassuming young woman, led a very sheltered, religious upbringing, living with her parents until her wedding day. She had only one future in her mind: wife and mother. She wanted to marry a religious man who would take good care of her and her children, and in return, she would make a comfortable home and a good life. She wanted the ideal Christian life. When she met Chris, MaryJane worked as a secretary. According to Michael Finkel, she spent every Wednesday proselytizing door to door for the Witnesses, and Chris, smitten, joined in, just to be near her. Apparently, Christian's smooth talk, handsome face, and charismatic nature assured her that their dreams melded perfectly.

Perhaps she should have paid closer attention. As they were seeing each other, Chris was caught stealing from his employer, which did not sit well with the church elders. They refused to let Chris and MaryJane marry in the church. He approached her father, smooth-talked him into giving them his blessings, and on March 13, 1993, in Huron High School auditorium, a minister married Christian Longo and MaryJane Baker.

In 1996, they joyously proclaimed that they were to have their first child. Zachery Michael Longo was born in February 1997, followed by Sadie Ann, fourteen months later. MaryJane quit her job to be the full-time mother she had always wanted to be. Eighteen months later, in October 1999, little Madison Jeanne joined the family. MaryJane focused entirely on the children, keeping them tidy and dressing them well.

This is where the trouble began.

Christian had an idea of himself, his family and his role as provider. He, too, wanted to live the ideal American dream. He needed to provide and provide well. MaryJane looked to him, their babies looked to him, and the pressure to keep up with his ideal began to build. He wasn't going to have a poor family, living in a rundown place. He wanted a new minivan every two years for MaryJane to drive. He wanted nice clothes, wanted the children to have good toys, wanted to take the family on nice vacations, and have all of those things that telegraphed "success" to the outside world. He deserved that. His family deserved that. Christian Longo was a master of justification, and he resented the lengths he had to go in order to provide what he considered to be the mere basics.

And what of MaryJane's involvement in Christian's petty crimes? All the evidence pointed to MaryJane turning a blind eye to Chris's machinations. According to later testimony, it was Chris' job to provide for his family. MaryJane was continually fed lies and half-truths about their situation. She carried on, blissfully ignorant. According to Carlton Smith of *Willamette Week*, she stayed home and tended the household, and her husband brought home the money, the cars, the things they needed. She asked no questions, or if she did, she asked the wrong ones, because Christian had begun his life of conning, scamming, stealing, and forging checks.

The Trouble Begins

In January of 2000, when baby Madison was only a couple of months old, Chris quit his job and opened Final Touch Construction Cleaning. The business cleaned up construction sites and made brand new buildings ready for tenancy. Business was good, but the payroll grew too fast, and soon he was forging checks on his customer's bank account and bouncing payroll checks.

On February 16, 2000, a "Jason Joseph Fortner" took a new red Pontiac Montana minivan from a car lot in Sylvania, Ohio, for a test drive. The salesperson photocopied the phony driver's license and handed him the keys. Later that day, the red Montana arrived in Ypsilanti, at the Longo's home, where Chris replaced its license plate with one from another car. He would pay for the car, he rationalized, as soon as his undercapitalized business's receivables gained ground on its payroll expenditures.

Things were not going well—already his crimes were escalating out of control—but instead of owning up to his bad boy behavior and cleaning up his act, he threw gasoline on the fire. According to Matt Sabo and Bryan Denson of *The Oregonian*, by spring of 2000, Chris had started an extramarital affair with another of the Jehovah's Witnesses. MaryJane found out. The perfect family was decaying from the inside out, and the vise Christian had designed was beginning to squeeze him.

Financial difficulties began to grow exponentially. He obtained a line of credit in the name of Joe Longo, his adoptive father, and ran up $100,000 of debt. He defaulted on other loans and was passing bad checks. He hired temporary workers and couldn't pay them. He stole two construction trailers and a forklift, and then sold the forklift. The used equipment dealer who bought it sued Chris when he learned the forklift had been stolen.

In June 2000, Chris was drowning in debt, and Wexford Builders, the main client of his construction cleaning business, wasn't paying him fast enough to keep the wolf from the door. Chris began to forge checks to himself from the Wexford account. Between mid-June to mid-July, he wrote six fake checks to himself for close to thirty thousand dollars and cashed them at various area banks. Wexford called the police.

On July 14, 2000, while trying to cash yet another bogus check, the bank called the police. Chris took off but left his ID behind. That afternoon, the police arrested him. Chris, ever the calm pacifist, readily admitted forging the Wexford checks, justifying his actions by Wexford's slow attention to the invoices Longo had sent them. He was only taking what was rightfully his.

MaryJane picked him up at the police station in the stolen red Montana van. According to Detective Fred Farkas, she was neither surprised nor upset by Chris' arrest. At first he wondered if she was in on the scam, but eventually concluded that she was not.

The justice system went easy on Chris, since he had no previous criminal history, he immediately admitted his crime and pled guilty, he seemed apologetic and remorseful, and he was the sole support of his family. He pled guilty to four counts of fraud, was sentenced to three years' probation, community service, and to pay restitution.

Chris was "disfellowshipped" from the Kingdom Hall of Jehovah's Witnesses. Disfellowship is another word for shunning, a practice considered archaic by most, but is a part of Jehovah's Witness ways. According to the Witnesses, shunning is an act of love intended to inspire repentance and a return to right living. For the Longos, especially MaryJane, this must have been a horrifically shameful thing; without her community, she had only her husband and children to cling to. With the disfellowshipping, Chris lost all his Witness employees, they lost all their friends, and even his family no longer spoke to him.

On the Run

It seems that for a year Chris tried to toe the line. But in May 2001, desperation set them on the move. The world was closing in; they no longer answered the phone because the only callers were collection agencies. Longo sold their little house in Ypsilanti, forged a driver's license, jumped probation, and with the $8,000 in realized equity, moved to a warehouse in Toledo, Ohio. He left behind a half dozen lawsuits, two warrants, and $60,000 in debts.

In Toledo, the Longos had the $8,000 in cash from the sale of their house, a stolen construction trailer, forklift, trailer and boat, along with the red Pontiac Montana van.

He was paying $1,650 a month in rent for the warehouse, which he was using as a showroom to sell the stolen wares. But a family of five is expensive, and he had no income until one of those high-ticket items sold. He went back to forging checks for a living.

He made a deal to sell the $32,000 forklift for $5,000, but the too-good-to-be-true deal made the buyer suspicious. He called the Toledo police, who came to the warehouse to investigate.

On Aug. 30, 2001, Sgt. Paul Hickey, supervisor of the

Toledo Police Department's stolen-vehicles section, arrived at the warehouse to find the forklift, along with a boat, boat trailer, construction trailer and a rental truck, and the red Montana. MaryJane and the kids were in the van, Sgt. Hickey realized in retrospect, packed and ready to leave.

True to his nature, Chris was calm and polite. The police checked serial numbers on the forklift and the rental truck, neither of which had been reported stolen. MaryJane seemed indifferent to the police presence. If she knew what Chris was up to, she remained aloof and silent.

By the time the police discovered that the forklift and construction trailer were indeed missing—not yet reported stolen—from a construction site, the Longos were long gone. Chris and his family had fled, along with the red Montana and the rental truck. Left behind were the stolen goods, along with boxes and boxes of the Longo's household possessions. Photo albums, clothing, toys, everything.

With no word from MaryJane for some time, her worried sisters decided to visit her, but when they arrived at the warehouse, it was empty.

No forwarding address.

They filed a missing persons report. They were afraid that something bad was about to happen.

Desperation Takes Hold

With MaryJane and the kids in the Montana and Chris in the rental truck, the Longos headed west. In a couple of days, they reached Sioux Falls, South Dakota. Chris rented a large storage locker, drove the rental truck half full of their household possessions inside, paid a month in advance, then jumped into the van with MaryJane and the children.

They continued west as far as they could go: the Pacific Ocean. They reached Yachats, Oregon, on September 12, 2001. Chris never considered it running away. He considered it making a change for the better. He'd make good on all those debts. He just needed a little breathing room.

The family stopped at Ocean Odyssey Vacation Rentals. Chris said he'd been transferred to a new job in Oregon, that his wife and children were beat from traveling and they needed to find a short-term rental. He'd pay cash.

He had cash, because he'd just pawned MaryJane's wedding ring.

According to Carlton Smith of *Willamette Week*, the people at Ocean Odyssey felt sorry for the Longos. An exhausted MaryJane held the baby on her lap and said almost nothing. The two older children were quiet and well-behaved. The Longos rented a modest house in Waldport for $300 a week. They pulled that off for a couple of weeks, but eventually, the money ran out and they had to move to a twenty-two dollar a night motel in Newport. Chris hated it. He hated having his family live in a "roachy" place and eat noodles for dinner. It went against every idea he had of himself, and how he would provide for his family. He'd get paid on Friday and be out of money by Tuesday, according to an interview published in *The Oregonian*.

"And now we're, we are pulling pennies out of the ashtray," Longo said. "Ah, to where that was almost empty. So, it just, it never got any better. It never got any better. I mean, we could get bread and ramen noodles," Longo said. "Which killed me. I mean we are used to eating whatever, going to the grocery store, spending $200 and not even thinking about it. And now we are trying to figure out how we can do it for five bucks."

Under such desperate circumstances, most people would take a serious look at where they are, where they want to be, and then make a plan for getting there. But Christian Longo didn't think that way. His plan was more dramatic. He had a better idea. Success begets success. The family moved out of the cheesy motel and into The Landing, an upscale condominium on Yaquina Bay in Newport.

On November 30, he negotiated the rent down to $1,200 a month—almost exactly his monthly pay working at Starbucks inside the Fred Meyer department store in Newport. Longo told the condo manager that he was working for Qwest and he would pay the rent as soon as a check arrived. Longo described the second-floor condo as a "perfect spot," a place with a kitchen and washer and dryer and fancy enough to have friends over. "It was everything we needed," Longo said.

They moved in, but Chris had no way to pay the rent that was currently due. Nor the following month's rent. Again, his life was built on lies.

On December 14 it all came crashing down. He came home from work about eleven-thirty, fixed himself something to eat, then stood in the rain on the balcony of their apartment. According to an interview with detectives Roy Brown of the Oregon State Police, and Ralph Turre of the Lincoln County sheriff's office, "We didn't have any groceries again," Longo said. "And it was just payday and we were out of money that week on Sunday. I was thinking that [my family] were in that situation too long with me," Longo said. "That, that they deserved much better. I didn't know if I could give it to them."

On that rainy night on the Oregon coast, Christian Longo broke down. He was financially and morally bankrupt. He came home from work to a home with the five mouths to feed, house and clothe, and he had no food, nothing but a trail of debt, deception and crime, and no prospects of paying the rent or buying groceries. The world had closed in on him. He'd been in that situation too long and taken his family on the wild ride with him. He knew they deserved better. They deserved better than he could provide, and based on his track record, he didn't think he could give it to him.

But there was a better place he could send them. They'd be better off, and the pressure would be lifted from his overburdened shoulders.

On December 18, employees at the motel where the Longo family had stayed for a while in November, found baby clothes, women's clothing, family photos, the Longo children's baby books and MaryJane Longo's Michigan identification in their dumpster. An employee at the motel left a message for

Chris at the Fred Meyer department store, where he worked at Starbucks. When the manager delivered the message that his family's photos and baby items had been found, Longo responded that his kids must have left some of their stuff when they moved.

He never picked up the belongings.

The next day, December 19, Longo told co-workers that MaryJane had been involved in a three-year affair. She had taken the children and moved home to Michigan. They would not be back.

Also, that day, a Dodge Durango was found missing from an auto dealership, just south of Portland. In its place was the stolen red Montana minivan Longo had been driving. Inside it were toys, sleeping bags, cell phones and diving gear. The van also had a book titled *Running from the Law*, and pillows—including one without a pillowcase.

The Unthinkable

Later that same day, December 19, 2001, four-year-old Zachery's body floated up in Lint Slough. After Sadie's body was found, police distributed posters with the children's retouched photographs, and the Longo's Newport babysitter immediately recognized the children. She and her husband went to the morgue and identified the two Longo children. The autopsy report said that the cause of death was "consistent with drowning."

When police went to the Longo's condominium, they found it empty.

The first people the police wanted to question were the parents, but they were not to be found. And where was the baby?

J. Reid Meloy, a forensic psychologist and author of *The Psychopathic Mind* and *Violent Attachments*, says that family murders occur as the result of a build-up of anger and frustration, which threatens to crush the fathers' already-fragile ego. They can't take failure or humiliation. With no way to relieve stress, they let the frustration and anger build until it explodes into violence. A defenseless family is usually an easy target and convenient outlet for the rage. Once it's over, these fathers, if they don't also kill themselves, often feel much better.

Two days after Christmas, divers raised two dark green suitcases from Yaquina Bay in Newport, Oregon, mere yards from the Longo's expensive apartment at The Landing. In one was the body of 110-pound MaryJane Longo, 34, forced into a fetal position and crammed into the suitcase. She had suffered a blunt trauma to the head and had been strangled. In the other was two-year-old Madison, wearing only a diaper. She, too, had been strangled.

That same day, Christian Longo boarded a flight in San Francisco, headed for Cancun, Mexico.

He'd been in San Francisco for a couple of days, long enough to apply for a job at a local Starbuck's. He put the Newport Starbuck's down as a reference. When the San Francisco manager called Newport, Newport employees called the police. The stolen van was found in the airport parking lot.

The Escape

In Mexico, Chris carried his own ID, didn't alter his appearance, and sometimes went by the name Michael Longo, his middle and last names. He stayed in Cancun while Lincoln County authorities charged him with seven counts of aggravated murder—the murder of a child under fourteen years of age carries two counts—but he didn't want to see any US newspapers or hear any news. He had determined that the pressure would be off, and so it was.

But one Canadian woman that he met in the $10/night hostel thought it was odd that one day he referred to himself as Mike and another time told her his name was Brad. Being carefree, he wasn't shy about his plans: he said that soon he intended to take off for Tulum, sixty miles south, to visit some Mayan ruins.

On January 5, four hundred people packed a flower-filled

Ypsilanti, Michigan high school auditorium to mourn the deaths of MaryJane and her three children. The funeral service was emotional for all involved. After the service, her father spoke with reporters who said that outside of her family, the church had always been the most important thing in MaryJane's life.

Meanwhile, Christian, outwardly freewheeling and blissfully ignorant of the Ypsilanti goings on, headed to Tulum on January 7, right after other hostel guests reported that their money had been stolen.

At some point, he decided to adopt the persona of Michael Finkel, a discredited journalist, formerly of *The New York Times*. He says he crafted the persona not because he thought police were looking for him, but because he didn't want to talk about himself. Longo had long admired Finkel's work; the journalist wasn't too famous, nor was he too obscure. Longo kept a notebook, told people in Tulum that he was researching Mayan ruins for a *New York Times* travel feature, and hooked up with a female photographer from Germany. Handsome, charming, charismatic Chris spun a dream of successful photographer and journalist traveling the world together, and instantly, he had a whole new life, complete with girlfriend. No debts. No pressure. No problems. He told her he was divorced; that he had no children. She was thrilled at her luck.

He began to believe that if he could fool his girlfriend into believing he was a real journalist, if he could fool their friends, perhaps he could fool an editor.

On January 11, Longo was added to the FBI's Ten Most Wanted list. The following day, "America's Most Wanted" television show aired a segment on him. John Walsh, series host, said, "He's very, very charming. He's very, very smart. He's very calculating. He's really, really good at disappearing."

The Canadian woman who had met Chris in Cancun saw the publicity, went to the FBI website, recognized Chris' photo, and called the FBI. Two FBI agents stationed in the Mexico City office went to Cancun, talked with local police and interviewed guests who may have come in contact with the fugitive. They printed posters with his photograph and circulated them on the Caribbean side of the Yucatan peninsula.

Meanwhile, in Tulum, Chris was living the life of the unburdened. He was drinking beer, smoking marijuana, snorkeling, dancing in a disco and sharing a rustic beach cabana with his new girlfriend. Those who met him saw him as a funny, articulate guy who seemed to come from money. He made friends easily, and he and his girlfriend were obviously in love.

Nobody had a clue as to his true nature.

The Capture

On a tip from a tour guide who'd seen the posters, FBI investigators and some twenty Mexican officials, including state and federal police and immigration officials, had Longo in surveillance on January 13 at the Tulum beach camp.

Early in the morning of January 14, Longo was relaxing at a beachside cabana with some English friends. They were drinking beer and passing around a joint when the police arrived, kicking in the door and making everyone lie down on the floor. Chris assumed it was a drug raid.

But one of the policemen referred to a photo and went directly to him. "Are you Christian Michael Longo?" As always, Chris was calm when confronted, and confirmed his identity. He was given the option of going back to the US immediately, or fight extradition, which meant he may have to spend up to six months in a Mexican jail. Longo opted to return to the US.

In searching Longo's cabana, police found one of his wife's credit cards, Argentine pesos—which they believed had been stolen from the hostel guests in Cancun—and a notebook in which he had taken notes about the Mayan ruins and other travels.

The police confiscated his belongings, and as they did, he didn't even cast a glance at his horrified girlfriend. He left the camp in handcuffs.

On January 23, 2003, his twenty-eighth birthday, Longo

was indicted on seven counts of aggravated murder.

As the country held its breath, Longo, in a move that surprised everyone, pled guilty to killing his wife and two-year-old Madison, and not guilty to killing the two older children.

The Trial

Christian Longo's murder trial began March 10, 2003. His amazing defense: his wife was the one who had the breakdown. She killed the two older children, throwing them off the bridge, then tried to smother Madison, but didn't complete the job. In a fit of rage, Longo murdered his wife, and then completed the job on the 2-year old, either to keep her from living a traumatic life, having seen her siblings murdered in cold blood, or to keep her from living a brain damaged life, having been half-strangled to death by her mother, it was never clear. Regardless, an odd defense, to be sure.

The prosecution contended that Longo thought his family was in his way and killed them to enjoy a more uninhibited, free-spending lifestyle than was favored by his careful, conservative Jehovah's Witness church. They presented a witness who saw a red minivan stopped on the Lint Slough bridge at about 4:30am on December 17. The witness spoke with the lone male occupant, to see if he needed assistance. The man said that he did not, and the witness went on his way.

Longo's court-appointed public defenders made no opening statement. Christian's testimony on the stand was his defense. According to *The Oregonian*, Longo said he wanted to "be on the stand for as long as possible to be able to air what needed to be aired, to be able to tell, unfortunately, what took place." He was in charge. His attorneys, it seemed, helplessly sat by to watch him hang himself.

His four-day testimony included his determination to never ask for money of family members, due to pride. "Pride has always been an issue for me," he said.

According to *The Oregonian*, Longo appeared relaxed and spoke easily, frequently smiling and occasionally laughing slightly in recounting his life through the birth of his third child, Madison. And then the testimony turned dark.

As MaryJane's grieving family looked on, Longo recounted that on December 17, he and MaryJane had an emotional, four-hour early morning discussion, in which he revealed his lies and crimes to her for the first time. Devastated, heartbroken by the deception, MaryJane had refused to communicate with him for the rest of the day.

That night, Longo testified, MaryJane picked him up from work at eleven p.m., wearing only her bathrobe. She turned away from him in the car and wouldn't speak. When they reached home, MaryJane was crying and mumbling, and then she backed up against the railing, refusing to go inside.

"That's when I started to get alarmed," Longo said. He hauled MaryJane into the apartment and she became hysterical, then fell to the floor. He ran through the condo, to find tiny Madison motionless on their bed. "I ended up grabbing her shoulders and shaking her, and she wasn't moving at all." He went back to MaryJane, picked her up and began shaking her violently against a hallway wall in an attempt to find out what had happened to Zachery and Sadie.

"She started to say, 'You did this to us. You did this. It's your fault,'" Longo testified. "It wasn't until she said, 'You killed us,' and that's when it became extremely difficult. That's when she said something about, 'They're by the house. They're in the water by the house,'" he said. "That's when I lost it."

With one hand on the lapel of her robe and the other hand around her neck, he lifted her off the floor and began squeezing, then dropped her. Then he grabbed her around the neck with both hands, lifted her off the floor and again began squeezing.

"I didn't stop until I couldn't hold her up anymore," Longo testified. Then he went to Madison and saw her chest move. During the course of a few minutes he said he watched her draw breaths periodically. He shook her again, trying to revive her, but she remained unresponsive.

"I didn't know what to do," Longo said. "Even though she

was breathing I thought of her as dead at that point." He said he put his hand on her throat to cut off her air supply and squeezed until "I knew she couldn't breathe anymore." And then he detailed putting their bodies into the suitcases, carrying them down the dock and throwing them into the bay.

In closing statements, the defense called to attention the fact that the bodies of MaryJane and Madison were twelve miles apart from the bodies of the two older children, indicating the distinct possibility of two murderers. All the evidence against Longo, they said, was circumstantial.

The Verdict

On April 7, 2003, an eight-woman, four-man jury deliberated only four hours and twenty minutes before finding him guilty of murdering Zachery and Sadie.

With this verdict, the jury had three options for sentencing: They could sentence him to death by lethal injection; life imprisonment—a so-called "true-life" sentence; or life in prison with the possibility of parole in thirty years.

On April 16, the same jury, after deliberating only six and a half hours, sentenced him to death by lethal injection.

Minutes later, Longo addressed the packed courtroom to publicly condemn his acts and say that he expected no forgiveness.

"They deserved the best, and that's something I didn't provide," he said. "I was the one, in fact, they needed protection from."

Journalist Michael Finkel established and carried on an astonishing year-long relationship with Longo after his arrest. At first intrigued by Longo's choice of his identity to usurp, the two fell into weekly telephone conversations and over a thousand pages of shared correspondence, in which Longo serves up several different post-verdict versions of who killed whom and when. One of these is a full confession of throwing the two children, still alive, off the Lint Slough bridge.

According to Michael Finkel, Longo carries horrible

memories that haunt him still.

One can't help but wonder if one of those memories had to do with being on the Lint Slough bridge, throwing away his two older children, perhaps still alive, perhaps screaming, "No, Daddy, please, no, Daddy, don't!" until the murky waters of the slough silenced them.

During his emotional post-sentencing statement, Longo said he did not fathom the enormity of his crime until he'd been jailed in Newport. While there, he saw newspapers and photos of the makeshift memorial that appeared on the bridge over Lint Slough.

"Up until then," he said, his chin trembling, "I was feeling an amazing amount of self-pity."

Longo remains on Death Row.

Bibliography

The Oregonian — "Hundreds go to service in Michigan for slain family" January 6, 2002

FBI Press Release — January 11, 2002

The Oregonian — "The Longo killings: A trail of crimes" January 12, 2002

CBS Worldwide, Inc. — "FBI Arrests Top Murder Suspect" Jan. 14, 2002

The Oregonian — "Longo Captured in Mexico" January 15, 2002

The Oregonian — "Tourists recall Longo's boasts, carefree ways" January 23, 2002

Michigan Free Press — "Charmer becomes murder defendant" January 26, 2002

The Oregonian — "Court documents in Longo case detail killings, disposal of bodies" March 23, 2002

Willamette Week — "The Life and Crimes of Christian Longo"

August 14, 2002

Willamette Week — "The Life and Crimes of Christian Longo" August 21, 2002

The Oregonian — "Longo recalls his family's final days in interview" December 3, 2002

The Register-Guard — "Cast out: Religious shunning provides an unusual background in the Longo and Bryant slayings" March 2, 2003

Associated Press — "Judge grants Longo one-week delay" March 13, 2003

The Oregonian — "Longo says that pride kept him from asking for help" March 27, 2003

The Oregonian — "Longo says wife was first to kill" April 2, 2003

The Oregonian — "Longo condemned to die" April 17, 2003

Newstar.com — "Family murder: It happens in the nicest homes" May 18, 2003

Ann Arbor News — "Christian Longo's Timeline" June 12, 2005

"The Journalist and the Murderer," Michael Finkel, *Vanity Fair*, June 2005

CrimeLibrary.com — "Fathers Who Kill" by Katherine Ramsland

True Story: Murder, Memoir, Mea Culpa by Michael Finkel — Harper Collins, 2005

The Psychopathic Mind and *Violent Attachments by* J. Reid Meloy — Jason Aronson, Inc., 1992

The Majesty of Maggots

Gil Grissom, from the CSI television show, always saw the big picture.

While the local police officers in some backward Nevada town stand around scratching their heads and staring at the headless corpse, Gil gets squinty-eyed, looking around at everything but the obvious. Then he pulls out a pair of tweezers, moves in close, and tenderly picks up a maggot.

A maggot!

Yuck.

Who among us can erase the mental imprint of the first time we saw something undeniably dead that seemed to be alive, it was so covered (and filled) with heaving masses of squirming maggots?

While endlessly fascinating to little boys (one summer, my brother had to make a daily pilgrimage to the vacant lot to check on the maggots' progress with a dead possum), little girls tend to find maggots no less than gag worthy.

I can't even eat orzo today.

While living in Hawaii, I once picked a friend up at the airport and took him back to his house. He had neglected to take out the garbage before he left for two weeks, and maggots were cascading out of the trash compactor, piled up in front of it, and spreading out across the kitchen floor.

I had never, I realized, gotten over the dead possum episode

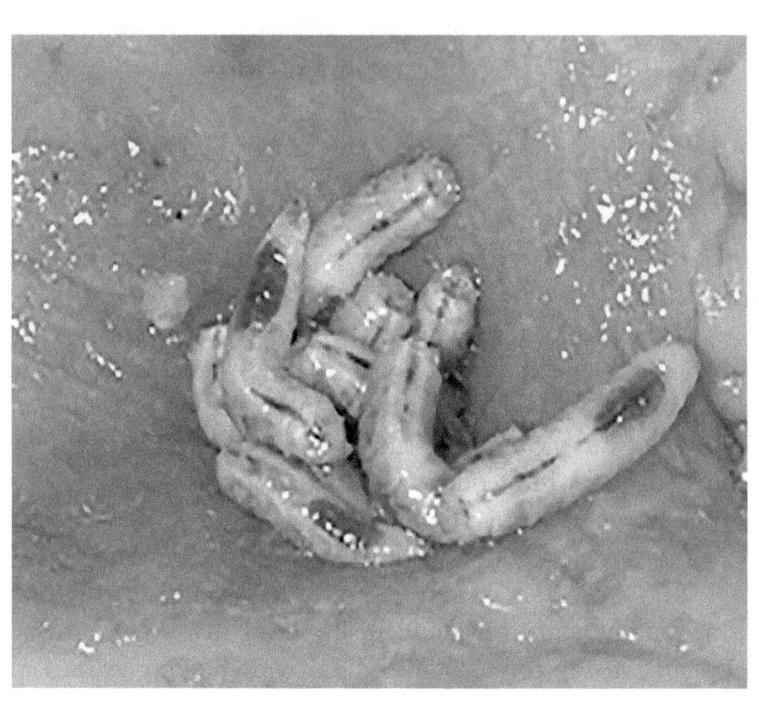

of my youth. I gagged and ran. The thought of staying to help him clean up never once entered my mind.

The only time I ever saw majesty in a maggot was when I watched a time-lapse film of a dead animal, a dog, I think, rotting in the sun. Reduced to sixty seconds or so, what the maggots accomplished was a thing of beauty. I didn't see rice-like worms feeding, squirming and oozing, I saw a sanitation system. They were efficient and effective in a dance of life and death and renewal.

Sheer poetry.

I'm certain that the human gag reflex when confronted with fly larvae is a good survival mechanism. Bugs are a good indication of food too past its prime to eat. In fact, until 1668, it was assumed that rotting meat *produced* maggots. Only when scientist Francesco Redi actually conducted experiments, was it confirmed that maggots were from flies.

And, while we're on the topic of maggots, Maggot Therapy is alive and well. Clinical studies are now being performed in hospitals using medicinal maggots (!) to debride necrotic tissue, sterilize wounds and stimulate healing. Doctors have known since the Civil War that soldiers who had maggot-infested wounds fared better in the long run than did those whose wounds festered and turned gangrenous. This idea fell out of favor when the miracle antibiotic drugs hit the market, but now we're turning back to larvae as perhaps the most efficient way to cleanse severely infected wounds.

In the end, we're all carrion.

As with all things, bugs have their place in the great scheme.

The first case of what we now call forensic entomology occurred near Paris in 1855, when the remains of a baby was discovered behind a plaster mantle in a house. The occupants were obviously under suspicion, but the investigator determined that the insects present on the corpse indicated the baby had died at least two years prior to discovery. The current occupants breathed a sigh of relief. They were cleared, and the previous occupants of the house charged.

I am a passionate gardener with huge compost bins. I keep red wiggler worms in a bin in my garage to eat my kitchen scraps. The worms take potato peels, celery leaves and overripe melon rinds and turn it all into garden gold. I throw leaves and weeds and coffee grounds into an outside compost bin and out comes the most wonderful soil, thanks to sow bugs and worms and beetles and fungi and things I can't even imagine.

I know all about the value of digestive bacteria and the critters who slurp up what they leave behind.

Nature eventually recycles everything.

Maggots, though, aren't welcome in my compost (or anywhere else in my life), so I don't invite them. They're carrion eaters, so there are no meat scraps in my bins.

Ah, but to a forensic entomologist, maggots are tools.

To Gil Grissom, CSI entomologist, they can be very revealing evidence.

Forensic entomology is one of the fastest growing sciences today, despite its humble beginnings in a now-famous murder case in 1235 A.D. China. A man was found murdered, slashed to death. The local investigator had all the villagers bring their sickles to town and lay them upon the ground.

Flies were attracted to only one of the tools, most likely because of human tissue remnants. The evidence was obvious, even to the guilty owner of that sickle. Even then, bugs pointed the condemning finger at the guilty party. He confessed.

Simply put, forensic entomology is the science of investigating insect activities as they interact with the legal system.

The legal system!

This definition surprised me. But then I remembered that not long ago I heard that "insane" is a legal term, not a medical one. That surprised me, too. I guess I'm still naïve enough to expect that science can still be merely for the sake of knowledge. But the legal system has infiltrated every aspect of our lives, our deaths, and is now the purpose for entire branches of science.

To take the definition of forensic entomology a step further, the field has been broken into three branches. The first is urban entomology, insect infestations of buildings, such as termites, bedbugs, spiders, silverfish, carpenter ants and such, and the pesticides that eradicate them. The second is stored products entomology, mostly weevils, moths, mites and beetles that infest and ruin stores of grain, corn, legumes (beans, lentils, peas), milled cereal products, flour, bran, macaroni and other pasta products, dried fruits, dried vegetables, cheese, and nuts. These "pantry pests" spoil far more than they eat—10% of the world's stores of foodstuffs, and as much as 40% in some tropical environments.

The third field of forensic entomology is medicolegal entomology, sometimes referred to "forensic medical entomology" and in reality, "medico criminal entomology" because of its focus on violent crime. This is the stuff of CSI.

The basics are this: insects have a customary life cycle. Their habits are strict, and their preferences are few. Carrion-eating blow flies (Calliphoridae) and flesh flies (Sarcophagidae) will infest a corpse within 24 hours, weather permitting. If there are open wounds, flies can arrive within minutes of death. It is on these carrion buffet tables that the female flies lay their eggs.

Carrion-eating flies generally go through three larval stages before pupating and emerging as adult flies. Each of these stages is brief and easily predicted, with factors such as temperature, humidity, and other environmental considerations factored in. Especially temperature. Maggots are cold-blooded; they don't grow well unless there's heat. Case in point: my friend's garbage in hot, humid, tropical Hawaii.

Maggots hatch from these fly eggs in large numbers and move around a corpse as a group, disseminating bacteria and secreting enzymes which enable them to consume virtually all of the soft tissue.

Investigators on a fresh crime scene can collect the eggs and incubate them to maturity to discern the age of the larvae and identify the species of fly (not easy—some microscopic differences in fly species produce significant differences in fly behavior). On more advanced cases (i.e. corpses having been allowed to ripen longer), several different types of larvae may be present, in differing life stages.

In what Grissom calls "Linear regression," the time of death (or PMI, "postmortem interval") can be determined by the type and age of insects on the body. Examine what insects are present, their current stage of life, and count backwards to when the first eggs were laid, factor in the ambient temperature, and you'll have the time of death.

It's not as easy as it seems. First of all, the first instar larvae, the stage that hatches directly from the egg, cannot be readily identified as to species. The second instar, or the next maggot stage, can only be correctly identified on occasion. And the third instar, or prepupal larvae, the largest maggot stage and the most commonly observed, is only valuable to a researcher if it is collected and preserved properly. Scanning electron microscopes are currently being used to refine maggot species identification.

Next, there's the climate. Wherever there is a corpse, there are fluctuating temperatures—warmer during the day, colder at night. Rainfall, cloud cover, wind speed and direction, and relative humidity all have a bearing on the speed with which maggots develop. Not only do fly species differ from region to region, from habitat to habitat, and from season to season, some come into their own in the coolest parts of the year, some in the warmest parts of summer, some like the bright sun, some like the shade. After all the soft tissue has been consumed, the maggots leave and the beetles move in to pick the bones clean.

So it isn't just a matter of picking up some maggots and pronouncing the time of death. It's an extremely complex puzzle, right up Gil Grissom's alley.

It can be quite confusing, except to Gaia, who seems to have it all figured out. A place for everything, our Mother Earth tells us in myriad ways, and everything in its place. She has no problem knowing which bugs to send to a crime scene, and in what order.

The Gaia Hypothesis was formulated in the 1960s by a British chemist named James Lovelock. He postulates that our planet functions as a single organism and maintains conditions necessary for its own survival. Named after Gaia, the Greek goddess of the Earth, Lovelock maintains that the world is a completely self-sustaining entity. He has written a series of books on the subject, and his theories are popular in environmental classes all over the world. While still a hypothesis, the concept provides many useful lessons about the interaction of physical, chemical, geological, and biological processes on Earth, and endless fodder for intelligent speculation.

It's all about seeing the bigger picture.

I think he's on to something.

But let's get back to maggots.

Horrible, grisly little critters.

And yet sublime.

Maggots not only tell crime scene investigators the time of death, but place of death. In "Grave Danger," a particularly gruesome and suspenseful CSI episode directed by Mr. Gruesome Suspense himself, Quentin Tarantino, Grissom and company couldn't find Nick Stokes, who had been buried alive. When Nick was attacked by fire ants, they had their first real clue. Fire ants live in moist soils, not in the Las Vegas desert. The team found him buried beneath the damp earth of a commercial plant nursery.

Certain flies are typical only in urban areas. When Grissom found musket flies on a body left in the woods, he knew the corpse had been moved from the city, the original site of the murder, where musket flies dwell. "They're the first witnesses to the crime," he said. "They're perfect. They're doing their jobs, exactly what God intended, recycling us back to the earth."

Bugs are Grissom's passion, having an apparent "entomology collection," and he even wanted to take a photograph of chigger bites for his "bite collection." I find this completely consistent with his character. He seems to be the one who always seeks out, and finds, the larger picture. He's the adult in charge, after all, and that means that he must have a wider view of everything: human nature, criminal behavior, co-worker relations, and the global consistency of insect activities.

I bet Grissom has a copy of Lovelock's book on his nightstand.

Let's set the large picture aside for the moment and get back to the grisly.

In 1994, Patricia Cornwall released a book called *The Body Farm*, alerting the world to an aromatic FBI "facility" in Knoxville, Tennessee, where at any one particular time, one might find dozens of human corpses lying about in the humidity. They are test subjects, and they are clothed and unclothed, buried and unburied, in the sun and in the shade, cooled, heated, sitting in a car, lying on metal shards. In many of the experiments, researchers are trying to duplicate crimes currently under investigation.

This is where the literal field research in forensic entomology is done.

By the way, if you want to donate your remains to the Body Farm, or the "Anthropology Research Facility" as it is officially called, you'll have to get in line. While at first they had to rely on unclaimed cadavers of homeless men, there is now a waiting list for those who name the Body Farm as their final resting place.

As creepy as all this may seem, it is in reality no different than the study of photosynthesis on a variety of plants, or the correlation of the phases of the moon to fish and animal activity. It's all the same system. Gaia seems to know exactly what she's doing. We're just bumbling along, trying to catch up.

As much as we like the criminal aspects of forensics, the larger application for forensic entomology is in civil court. Maggot infested meat, for example, is a common complaint. Did whoever buy it leave it sitting on the counter too long before putting it away? Or did it really come that way from the butcher's counter?

In one landmark case, a 188-kilo shipment of marijuana

was seized, and by plotting on a map the home turf of the sixty-one species of insects found therein, investigators were able to determine the country of origin, and the dealers were indicted not only for possession, but for international trafficking.

And then there's the very disturbing suit against a funeral home who failed to properly embalm a client. As the wake progressed, maggots began to stream out of the deceased's nose.

Not nice.

As with any new leap in forensic science, old cases are being reopened and reevaluated, due to the new light being shed on entomological evidence.

But even so, knowing too much can sometimes be a confusing burden. There was a case of DNA being found so far away from a crime scene that it almost sank the investigation. Turned out to be fly specks. Flies that had feasted on the deceased's blood had congregated by the window, as flies are wont to do, and their excrement included the victim's DNA.

For all the press that forensic entomologists are getting these days, it's a pretty tiny universe of professionals, and they're rarely out in the field doing the fun stuff, like picking maggots from a slushy corpse. According to the American Board of Forensic Entomology, the most current worldwide directory shows only sixty-two forensic entomologists, a mere dozen practicing in the United States. Thirty-three of the sixty-two work solely with the medicolegal subdiscipline, and five more say that medicolegal entomology is only one of their specialties. The remaining twenty-four teach entomology or biology and/or are involved with research. Those working in the field spend most of their time training crime scene investigators to properly recognize, obtain and preserve evidence. Then they review said evidence, render their findings and regularly appear as expert witnesses in court.

Specimens are collected in the field by crime scene technicians, medical examiners or forensic pathologists, but the skill in correctly identifying each species of crime scene insect resides with a fully qualified entomologist.

It's got to be a calling.

Perhaps we all have our callings. We each seem to fit, somehow, into our communities. And our families.

Perhaps we're a more integral part of Gaia than we know.

Salmon swim upstream to spawn and then die in order to feed the bears who fertilize the forests. A salmon, it is said, can smell the difference between a worm from its spawning grounds and any other worm, amidst all those billions of gallons of rushing river water.

The weather patterns of our planet would be vastly different if it were not cocked precisely 23 degrees on its axis. Or if we had no moon. Perhaps Earth would be uninhabitable for life as we know it.

These things are not accidents.

And the expert housekeepers—the things that keep it all tidy—are the insects.

The fact that there are armies of arthropods ready, willing, and able to recycle our sloughed off mortal remnants is no less of a miracle, and no less a piece of the entire, complex ecosystem.

What's fun about it is that we're just beginning to discover the beauty in its intricate dance.

The closer a thing is examined, the more exquisite it becomes.

And the bad guys? The despicable heathens who commit murder for no rational excuse and then try to get away with it? Are they part of the whole ecological system too?

I don't know.

Personally, I think that of all the bugs that populate this planet, murderers are the ones that Gaia wants to swat.

She does not want the bad guys to get away with it, and she gives us all the tools we need to catch 'em.

We're just learning how to work with her.

Jeremy Bryan Jones: Meth Monster

A Series of Unsolved Murders

On Halloween night in 2002, thirty-eight-year-old Tina Mayberry stepped out of Gipson's restaurant in Douglasville, Georgia where she'd been attending a Halloween party dressed as Betty Boop. Moments later, she staggered back into the bar, bleeding from stab wounds and seeking help. Despite frantic efforts of party goers and the paramedics, she died a short time later at an Atlanta hospital. She had neither been robbed nor sexually molested; there was no apparent motive, no clues, no suspect.

In March 2003, sixteen-year-old Amanda Greenwell disappeared. Her badly decomposed body was discovered a month later, stabbed, her neck broken. Again, no motive, no clues, no suspect.

According to James Alan Fox and Jack Levin, in their book *The Will to Kill*, "One of the most striking and intriguing aspects of serial murderers is the nature of their motivation. Although it has been loosely described as 'motiveless,' there is indeed one—to satisfy an intense appetite for power and sadism. The serial murderer tends to kill not for love, money, or revenge, but just for the fun of it—because it makes him feel good."

A Missing Mom

Then on April 15, 2004, Patrice Endres showed up at her beauty salon like any other day. As usual, she was upbeat and smiling, and joking with the customers. She had left a love note on her husband's car that morning that read, "The best is yet to come." The mother of a sixteen-year-old boy by a previous relationship, Patrice was totally devoted to her husband and son.

When a customer arrived for her noon appointment, Patrice's salon, Tamber's Trim-N-Tan, was empty. The front door was unlocked, her purse and keys were on her desk, her lunch was in the microwave, and her car was out in front, parked at an odd angle. But the cash drawer was empty. Patrice had disappeared without a trace.

Endres' past had been a tough one, including a substantial drug history. According to the *Atlanta Journal and Constitution*, she had worked long and hard to quit messing with drugs and turn her life around. She'd gone back to school to learn the beauty trade, opened her own hair and tanning salon, married Rob Endres, and the two had plans to buy a bed and breakfast in Flagler, Florida. Life was good.

Over the protests of her family and friends, who say she was happier than she had ever been, police could find no motive for anyone to do anything to Patrice. Sometimes those with a history of drug abuse can hear the echoes of those drugs calling from a long distance. Police became convinced she had run off.

But Patrice's husband Rob knew better. He held a series of car washes to fund a reward for her safe return, which eventually reached $17,000. He plastered the town with posters with Patrice's photo, and the police station was flooded with over seven hundred leads. Air and ground searches revealed nothing. Rob worked tirelessly for months, searching for his bride.

A witness said she saw a man in a white cargo van blocking the entrance to Patrice's salon on the morning she disappeared. Community-wide searches went on from Coal Mountain to all the way to Matt. But community energy like that is hard to sustain, and around Christmas, the posters began to come down, along with the reward fund collection boxes. There still were no clues. Not a single lead had panned out.

This was not the first time a woman had gone missing in a grisly trail of terror. Rob Endres had no idea that his wife's disappearance was just the latest in a long line of murders, which had begun a decade earlier.

In Baxter Springs, Kansas, on May 11, 1992, twenty-year-old Jennifer Judd was stabbed to death with a long-bladed knife in the kitchen of her own home. Justin Judd, her husband of only ten days, found her body. Her keys were on the living room floor, and the lunch she had packed to take to him was in the front seat of the car.

At that state of the forensics art, there were no clues left at the crime scene. There was no apparent motive, and no suspects.

The Body Count Grows

On June 28, 2004, the decomposed torso of a young prostitute was found near Wright City, Missouri. Passers-by told investigators that they saw a white utility van at the rest stop off Interstate 70, near where the torso was found.

The unidentified woman was buried during a ceremony, complete with flowers, prayer and a few mourners who stood in place of the woman's unknown family members.

And then, On Sept. 18, 2004, family members found 45-year-old Lisa Nichols from Turnerville, Alabama, a divorced mother of two daughters, dead in her bathroom. She had been raped, shot three times in the head, and set on fire.

A Deadly FBI Error

John Paul Chapman was a good looking, charismatic guy living in a Douglasville, Georgia trailer park, where he continually found himself in trouble with the law. He fancied himself quite the ladies' man, but as with most alcoholics and addicts, his addiction always came first, and under the influence he did some bad things.

He'd been arrested for drugs, for indecent exposure, and for trespassing. His neighbors remembered him as being a scary kind of a guy, paranoid from drugs and alcohol, always worried that the police were closing in on him.

Every time he was arrested, his fingerprints were sent to the FBI, and they came back only as matches to his previous arrests in Georgia.

This eventually proved to be a very costly error.

One neighbor, who played cards and drank regularly with the good-looking Chapman, mentioned once that prayer might help John with his problems. He even suggested that they pray together.

It was a bad suggestion.

Chapman flipped out, saying he couldn't handle prayer in his house.

He was indeed a scary guy. Young Amanda Greenwell had lived in, and disappeared from, the same trailer park.

Nobody had any idea that John Paul Chapman was anything but a small-time druggie doing small time crime, because the FBI's fingerprint database failed to confirm his true identity.

"Law enforcement lost an opportunity to prevent further criminal activity by this individual," the FBI later said in a statement, according to the *Chicago Tribune.*

"Law enforcement agencies across the country submit roughly fifty thousand fingerprint comparison requests a day to the FBI system which contains forty-five million sets of prints. Given the size of the system, some errors are bound to occur," said the editor of the *Journal of Forensic Identification.*

Like more than eighty percent of the fingerprints submitted to the database facility in West Virginia, Chapman's fingerprints were submitted as digital images. Sometimes the quality of these images can be a problem, leading to errors—either false identifications, such as the implication of an Oregon lawyer in the Madrid train bombings in 2004, or as in this case, the failure to correctly identify John Paul Chapman.

Jeremy Bryan Jones

Jeremy Bryan Jones grew up in a middle-class home in Miami, Oklahoma, where his mother was a florist, and his father a woodshop supervisor.

He had trouble in high school and was transferred to a school in Quapaw because of discipline problems in Miami. He went to school for a short time before dropping out.

Jeremy Jones' first run-in with the law was in January of 1990, when he was sixteen years old. He was charged with assaulting a boy, and when the boy's mother came to his defense, Jones assaulted her as well, according to the *Joplin Globe*.

One of Jones' high school schoolmates was Justin Judd, and Jones eventually lived next door to Judd for a while.

Jones was a problem neighbor, according to Judd. "We called the police on him several times," Judd said. "You could hear his wife or girlfriend screaming all of the time. The police would show up and she would say: 'Nothing's wrong.' And the police would leave."

In 1992, Justin Judd's bride Jennifer was murdered, stabbed to death in her own kitchen.

Jones' first rape charge came on November 5, 1995. He was charged with rape a second time on January 10, 1996, along with the unlawful possession of meth. The following day he held a loaded revolver to a woman's vagina and threatened to shoot her. This charge included sexual battery.

He spent time at the Dick Conner Correctional Center in Hominy, Oklahoma, where he sobered up and felt bad about his drug-fueled crimes.

On March 3, 1997, he pleaded guilty to three charges of sexual battery and received a five-year sentence of probation. The two girlfriends he raped were afraid to testify. His court-mandated sex-offender counseling sessions didn't go well, and he was ultimately kicked out. He flat-out ignored the two court-ordered requests for DNA samples.

On October 19, 2000, a warrant was issued for his arrest for probable cause. His probation was being revoked.

He sold his truck and hit the road with the proceeds. He left Oklahoma on the run.

A Convenient New Identity

In Joplin, Missouri, Jones met the mother of a Missouri prison inmate. He was complaining to her that the system was out to get him, and she loaned him her son's identity: John Paul Chapman. He spent his time on a bus from Joplin to Tuscaloosa, Alabama, memorizing his new identity, complete with social security number and birth date.

He drifted, working as a delivery driver, a construction worker, and whatever else he could find, from Oklahoma to Atlanta. A bounty hunter tracked him to Tuscaloosa, so he went to Mobile, Alabama, looking for work as a laborer, hoping to stay one step ahead of his past and earn some quick cash helping to rebuild in the aftermath of Hurricane Ivan. He found employment and lodging with an empathetic and religious home builder and his family.

But walking the straight and narrow wasn't his style, and he soon found himself back on the street. His silver tongue and good looks soon found him fresh lodgings with another casual acquaintance and his family, but his presence made the wife very nervous. It wasn't long before he was kicked out again.

A Monster on the Loose

One of his former roommates believes Jones had it in for women. "He was always saying derogatory things about women, about putting them in their place, about smacking them down," she said. One of his favorite jokes was, "What do you tell a woman with two black eyes? Nothing—you done told the bitch twice."

People either loved him or were repelled by him, yet his self-image remained untarnished. "I'm a likeable guy," he said in a recent interview. "I'm the guy next door."

But a former roommate saw his darker side. "The monster came out when he was on meth." The monster seemed to be an increasingly larger part of his personality.

According to Peter Vronsky, in his book *Serial Killers: The Method and Madness of Monsters*, "Serial killers, although often described as monsters, rarely appear to be creatures with blood dripping from their fangs or crazed psychopaths babbling satanic rituals. While a few are exactly like that, many appear at first glance to be healthy, normal, and even attractive people. And that is precisely the problem—with a serial killer, a victim rarely gets beyond the first glance. Others are simply invisibly unmemorable and unnoticeable, until somebody notices them killing."

On Halloween in 2002, Jones went to Gipson's, a favorite bar in Douglasville, where a Halloween party was in full swing. Monsters other than those with plastic masks were apparently out that night, because at midnight, Tina Mayberry stumbled in from the parking lot, and then died from her stab wounds.

A Break in the Nichols Case

In September 2004, when family members found 45-year-old Lisa Nichols, a divorced mother of two daughters, dead in her bathroom, the community came alive to help solve the murder. Lisa had been raped, shot three times in the head, then set on fire.

From the beginning, neighbors were helpful. One remembered seeing a vehicle parked outside Nichols' home; another recalled part of the license tag number.

Quickly, the evidence led police to a man known as "Oklahoma."

A man who employed "Oklahoma" as a laborer, gave police his full name as he knew it: John Paul Chapman. He also provided authorities with a Social Security number and a birth date.

Now police had a suspect.

Four days later, Detective Burch, the lead detective investigating Nichols' murder, got a call on his cell phone.

It was John Paul Chapman.

An incredulous Burch kept Chapman talking on the phone while his partner traced the call.

They talked about this and that, even the weather.

Twenty minutes later, police surrounded the suspect, who was inside a house not far from where Nichols had been killed.

He was still on the phone with Detective Burch.

Police charged him with capital murder, rape, burglary and kidnapping in Nichols' death.

Linking the Two Identities

Police were happy to have him in custody, but the seriousness of the situation had yet to come to light.

As a matter of procedure, Burch had Chapman's fingerprints run through the FBI's database, the Integrated Automated Fingerprint Identification System.

This database holds more than 200 million sets of prints, and is tapped more than 50,000 times each day by law enforcement agencies around the world.

The AFIS data on John Paul Chapman came back naming the John Paul Chapman alias he had been using—even though Jeremy Bryan Jones' fingerprints had been in the system since 2000, when he skipped bail in Oklahoma.

Obviously, the FBI later admitted, there was a glitch.

This attempt was the fourth time the AFIS failed to match Jones' true identity to his original prints—a mistake that apparently had deadly consequences.

Between October 2003 and June 2004, Jones, posing as John Paul Chapman, was arrested three times in Georgia on minor offenses.

All three times, authorities sent his prints to the FBI, but the computer system never made a match. Had the match been made, local authorities said, Jones would have remained in jail.

Instead, he was released, and police say he killed four more women: Katherine Collins, whose body was found in New Orleans on Feb. 14, 2004; Amanda Greenwell, a 16-year-old Douglas County girl whose body was found in April 2004;

Patrice Endres, a hairdresser who vanished on April 15, 2004; and Nichols, found in her Alabama home in September, 2004.

Jones was charged in the deaths of Collins, Greenwell and Nichols. He remains a suspect in the Endres slaying.

The FBI Admits Their Mistake

In response to queries by *The Atlanta Journal-Constitution*, the FBI admitted that a mistake occurred with its database and is now investigating the errors and making certain the database is working properly.

If Jones had been arrested in Mobile on a minor offense like before, chances are, they would have set him free to kill yet again.

But this time, facing murder, rape and other charges in the death of Lisa Nichols, the suspect was held without bond.

Still naïve about the true identity of the man they had in jail, detectives sent out a routine national teletype, just in case Chapman was wanted in other states for other crimes.

Missouri responded, saying they knew a John Paul Chapman with the same social security number and birth date, but that man had been in their prison since 1999. They sent along a photograph of their inmate and a set of his fingerprints.

Neither one matched the man in custody in Mobile.

For a week, police worked around the clock, trying to figure out the puzzle.

And then the suspect himself gave them a clue.

Good Police Work

John Paul Chapman made several telephone calls from the jail's pay phone to a number in Miami, Oklahoma. The phone number belonged to a Jeanne Beard.

A Miami detective told the Mobile police that he knew Mrs. Beard, and knew there were outstanding warrants for her son.

His name?

Jeremy Bryan Jones.

The Miami detective sent Jones' photos and fingerprints to Mobile, along with the outstanding warrants. This time, said Marvin Whitfield, a crime scene investigator with the Mobile County Sheriff's Office, the prints matched.

Chapman was surprised, to say the least, when presented with the outstanding warrants for Jeremy Bryan Jones, and evidence of his duplicate identities.

Jailhouse Confessions

While awaiting trial for the rape and murder of Lisa Nichols, Jones confessed to killing as many as eight women in metro Atlanta, including five prostitutes. He gave specific detailed confessions to police in private but maintained his innocence in the presence of his mother and his girlfriend. He detailed the crimes, including the victims' names and the locations of the killings. Mobile Sheriff's Detective Paul Burch said Jones was "very nonchalant and matter-of-fact" in recounting the rapes and killings.

The more Jones talked, the higher the body count began to grow. By November, the count was up to thirteen victims of which ten were women. Then seventeen. Then twenty-one, in five states.

Jones passed a polygraph where he talked of picking up prostitutes on stretches of Atlanta streets lined with strip clubs and dumping their bodies in wooded areas and once, off a bridge into a river. He even sketched a rough map of the locations where he committed crimes in Alabama, Georgia, Oklahoma and Kansas that dated back to 1992.

Jones had lots more to say. He bragged at one time that he could "talk the panties off a nun." He thought of himself as a ladies' man and considered himself to have been born lucky—until the meth got hold of him. He also mocked the authorities who arrested him three times in Georgia, since they failed to match his fingerprints, and set him free.

Douglas County Sheriff Phil Miller said they were going to approach his confessions with cautious optimism. "Jeremy

Jones has confessed to the deaths of Tina Mayberry, Patrice Endres and Amanda Greenwell," he said. "There is some evidence to support the Greenwell confession, but almost no evidence to support his confessions in the Endres or Mayberry cases."

On February 14, 2004, Katherine Collins, 45, was found stabbed to death in New Orleans. Jones has been charged in that killing.

On December 30, 1999, Danny and Kathy Freeman of Welch, Oklahoma, were shot to death, possibly to settle a drug debt. The killer set fire to their home. The same night, their 16-year-old daughter, Ashley, and her friend Laura Bible, disappeared. Jones admitted to murdering the girls, and said he threw their bodies down a mine shaft.

Jones also admits stopping at Tamber's Trim-N-Tan salon, high on meth and needing directions. When he found Patrice Endres, an attractive petite brunette, alone in the shop, he said he kidnapped, raped and killed her, dumping her body off a bridge in Douglas County.

After his capture, he seemed eager to talk to anyone who would talk with him, trading interviews and confessions for visits with his family and his girlfriend. Investigators from Oklahoma, Georgia, Louisiana and California traveled to Mobile to talk with him.

His court-appointed attorney, Habib Yazdi, dismissed all his confessions. "He will talk to anyone and confess to anything if they'll let him talk to his mother and his girlfriend for hours. He's getting fancy lunches with crab claws and dinners and drinks. Then he later says it's all false."

ADA Furman said that the charismatic Jones was thriving on the national media attention, including segments on the Today show, CNN, Fox News and "A Current Affair."

His Girlfriend

Vicki Freeman, Jeremy Jones' girlfriend, continues to believe in him. She says that the police have it all wrong.

"He's a wonderful man," she said. "He's caring, considerate, loving. Gentle." Freeman, fourteen years Jones' senior, met him in 2003 in the same bar where Tina Mayberry was stabbed. Jones approached her and told her she was beautiful. It was apparently love at first sight.

But love with Jeremy Jones has a dark side, and Freeman admits that he had been physically abusive, but that they always made up. She thinks that the police are piling all their old crimes on her lover, trying to clear their books of unsolved murders "for brownie points."

"He's a low-rent Ted Bundy," Assistant DA John Furman said in Mobile. "Otherwise reasonably smart women somehow find him interesting. He doesn't look like a monster. Obviously, Vicki Freeman is playing with fire."

She only knew him as John Paul Chapman until his arrest. She'd called the police on him at least twice, once when she was afraid for her life, after which she declined to press charges, and another time, after he reportedly shot up two grams of meth and was trying to kill himself.

When he and Freeman moved into an apartment together in September 2003, Jones chatted up the neighbors, attracted to their eighteen-year-old daughter. The police arrested him for exposing himself to the girl, and repeatedly trying to enter her apartment after her parents had left for the day. Outside the daughter's bedroom window, the girl's parents found a box containing binoculars, rope, and tape.

After Hurricane Ivan, Jones moved to Mobile to find construction work. "I wanted to come down here, live on the beach happily ever after," he said. He phoned Freeman to tell her that he'd found work. She was pleased at the news, told him to get a place for them to live, and she'd be down to join him.

He made that phone call from Lisa Nichols' telephone. The next day, Lisa Nichols was dead—raped, shot, and set on fire.

Public Recantations

Jones has since denied that he killed anyone despite his public confessions, he faults the FBI for failing to discover his true identity and as a result, he has been labeled a serial killer. He even denies confessing to any killing.

Prosecutors speculated this about-face was a prelude to an insanity defense.

According to John Douglas, in his book *Journey into Darkness*, "[Serial killers and sexual predators] do what they do not because they need to eat or to keep a family from starving, or even to support a drug habit. They do it because it feels good, because they want to, because it gives them satisfaction. You can make the argument that many of them are compensating for bad jobs, poor self-image, mistreatment by parents, any number of things. But that doesn't mean we're going to be able to rehabilitate them.

"My colleague Greg McCrary uses the analogy of the cake. You've baked this chocolate cake which smells great and looks terrific, but as soon as you bite into it, you realize something is very wrong. Then you remember, 'Oh yeah, in addition to the eggs and flour and butter and cocoa, I recall mixing in some axle grease from my workshop. That's the only problem with the cake—the axle grease! If I can just figure out a way to get the axle grease out of the cake, it will be perfectly fine to eat.'

"This is the way I view rehabilitation of sexual predators, particularly serial sexual predators. The fact is that in the vast majority of cases, the urges, the desires, the character disorders that make them hurt and kill innocent men, women and children are so deeply ingrained in the recipe of their makeup that there is no way to get out the axle grease."

The Trial

During the trial, Jones blamed Lisa Nichols' neighbor for her death, but he said in other statements that he killed Lisa and burned her body while high on methamphetamines. He said, "It was like a nightmare. I was in a movie. I was higher than I had ever been in my whole life."

Alabama Attorney General Troy King said Jones "targeted his prey like any predator" and never showed even an ounce of remorse. Lead prosecutor Assistant Alabama Attorney General William Dill called Jones a classic sociopath. He said Jones testified at length and talked about Nichols and her family but "never shed one tear." However, when he spoke about his own mother, he bawled.

Defense attorney Greg Hughes sought a life sentence without parole, saying Jones suffered "extreme mental and emotional problems," including long-term drug addiction.

Jones was convicted on October 26, 2005 of rape, burglary, sexual abuse and kidnapping during capital murder, in the slaying of Lisa Nichols.

The Sentence

A twelve-person jury deliberated only thirty-five minutes before voting 10-2 for Jeremy Bryan Jones to be put to death.

Circuit Judge Charles Graddick, not bound by that recommendation, called Jeremy Bryan Jones "A danger to civilized society," as he sentenced him to die by lethal injection.

Jones told the court "God will have the final say," before Graddick sentenced him.

An appeal is automatic. Jones contends his confessions in the Nichols killing and others were just lies to get extra jail privileges like phone calls to family and meals. He vows to beat his case on appeal.

He has yet to face charges in Georgia for the March 2004 killing of 16-year-old Amanda Greenwell of Douglas County.

"One day I'll be a free man," Jones said. "I'll write me a book and laugh my ass off."

Jones remains on Death Row.

Bibliography

Journey into Darkness, John Douglass (Scribner, 1977)

Serial Killers: The Method and Madness of Monsters, Peter Vronsky (Berkley, 2004)

The Will to Kill, James Alan Fox and Jack Levin (Abacon, 2001)

The Atlanta Journal and Constitution — "The Life of a Killer" 12/4/05

The Atlanta Journal and Constitution — "Forsythe County" 12/18/05

WPMI-TV — "Suspected Serial Killer" 10/11/05

About.com — "A Psychological Profile"

The Atlanta Journal and Constitution — "Mobile 'sociopath' gets death 12/2/05

AP Worldstream — "Suspected serial killer sentenced" 12/1/05

AP Online — "Suspect in Ten Killings Gets Death" 12/1/05

The Atlanta Journal and Constitution — "Skeptical Eye Cast on Confessions 11/3/05

AP Worldstream — "Alabama investigators Say Convicted" 11/2/05

AP Online — "Ala. Killer Admits to 12 More" 11/1/05

The Atlanta Journal and Constitution — "Killer Talks of 8 Dead" 11/2/05

The Atlanta Journal and Constitution — "Alleged Serial Killer Convicted" 10/28/05

The Atlanta Journal and Constitution — "Tracking A Murder Suspect" 5/13/05

The Atlanta Journal and Constitution — "Suspected Serial Killer Also Angry" 5/7/05

AP Worldstream — "FBI Database Botched Fingerprint Check" 5/5/05

Morning Edition (NPR) — Profile: FBI Faces Criticism 5/5/05

St. Louis Post Dispatch — "FBI Blames Computer Foul-Up" 5/5/05

Chicago Tribune — "Fugitive Freed by FBI Computer Error" 5/5/05

The Atlanta Journal and Constitution — "Suspect Told Tale of Random Evil" 4/5/05

The Atlanta Journal and Constitution — "A Charming Killer" 3/20/05

The Atlanta Journal and Constitution — "Rising Waters Halt Search" 3/11/05

Joplin Globe — "Alabama Inmates had Ties to Slain Woman" 1/8/05

St. Louis Post Dispatch — "Possible Suspect Surfaces" 10/25/04

The Ojibwe News — "Police say DNA May Link Alabama Suspect 10/15/04

The Atlanta Journal and Constitution — "Douglas County Eyes Suspect 10/9/04

The Atlanta Journal and Constitution — "Where's Patrice?" 9/19/04

The Atlanta Journal and Constitution — "Husband Ups Ante" 6/17/04

The Atlanta Journal and Constitution — "Law and Order" 11/4/02

Joel Patrick Courtney:

A Horrifying Progression of Sex Offenses

Vanished!

On the morning of May 24, 2004, Brooke Wilberger, a beautiful blonde, blue-eyed coed who had just completed her freshman year at Brigham Young University, was washing lampposts in the Corvallis, Oregon apartment complex managed by her sister and brother-in-law. One moment she was there, the next moment, she was gone. She left behind her flip flops, a pail of sudsy water, and no witnesses to her disappearance.

Brooke, an honor student, athlete, a devout Mormon, and an integral part of her church community, was last seen wearing a hooded sweatshirt, a gray BYU t-shirt, dark blue jeans, small hoop earrings, maybe a silver watch, and a ring with "CTR" engraved on it (Choose The Right—a Mormon tradition). She was 5'4" and weighed 105 pounds. She had a scar from a gymnastic accident that extended from her wrist to her elbow on her right forearm.

When police arrived at the apartment complex, they found her sandals askew, leading them to suspect a struggle. Her purse, keys and other personal items were left in her sister's apartment, and her car was still in the parking lot.

It was clear to everyone involved that whatever had happened, Brooke did not leave the parking lot willingly.

Only one man saw something. His name was Brian, and he called the police, saying he'd seen a green minivan driving erratically. Before he could explain further, the call was disconnected, and he never called back. It was a tiny bit of information, just one of too many tips from helpful citizens.

The Community Gets Involved

The community rallied. Brooke grew up in Veneta, Oregon, a very small town of only 3,000 people, thirty miles south of Corvallis, itself a university town of only 50,000. Among friends, schoolmates, hometown folk and the LDS church family, within days, over four thousand flyers with Brooke's picture covered the area and reached every state in the union. Being prepared for an emergency is one of every Mormon's goals, and they were certainly prepared to get the word out about Brooke.

Her photo showed up on huge bulletin boards by the Interstate, and on buses all over the county. Public Service announcements showed up on television. Every gas station, every café, every convenience store had her flyer in the window. They held vigils. They held press conferences. They went on America's Most Wanted television show. Brooke's parents were featured on Good Morning America. Local real estate agents and property managers searched vacant properties and outbuildings. They held self-defense classes for women. At nineteen, Brooke was too old for the Amber Alert system for missing children, but as several high-profile cases recently have shown us, media pressure keeps the case alive. And those who loved Brooke were prepared to keep the pressure on.

Police received over eleven hundred tips, including four hundred from psychics. Theories abounded, stretching to the idea of Brooke being kidnapped and sold into white slavery in some exotic location.

Six hundred and fifty volunteers searched four thousand acres of field and woodlands around the Corvallis area. They searched the rivers and wetlands in canoes and kayaks. They searched the mountains on horseback.

But Oregon is vast and relatively unpopulated. There are thousands of acres of woodlands. Thousands of acres of wilderness.

A website, www.findbrooke.com was established with a downloadable flyer in a variety of languages; in the first twenty-four hours, the site received 26,000 hits. Brooke's disappearance hit a nerve with Americans and news of her abduction spread like wildfire.

Police began to focus in on four "persons of interest," but in the tumult, Brian's tip, of seeing the erratic green minivan, was almost entirely overlooked.

A "Person of Interest"

Eventually, the eye of the hurricane focused on Sung Koo Kim, a thirty-year-old man living with his parents in Tigard, Oregon, eighty miles north of Corvallis. Kim, who graduated from Washington State University in 2001 with degrees in Genetics and Cellular Biology, had been arrested ten days before Brooke's disappearance on suspicion of stalking an Oregon State University student. Oregon State is located in Corvallis.

The female student of his obsession was a member of the OSU swim team and frequented the Oak Park Apartments, where Brooke was staying with her sister. At first glance, the swim team member looked much like Brooke. When he was arrested, Kim had a copy of the woman's photo and her bio from the OSU website, along with a bag of dryer lint from the Oak Park Apartments.

That wasn't all they found when police searched his room in his parents' home. They also found 3400 pair of women's panties, collected from seven different colleges in the state, 40,000 photos of violent pornographic pictures of women being tortured and raped, and 4,000 pornographic videos. According to Jeff Lesowski, deputy Washington County district attorney, while some of the pornographic images were of children, the vast majority were of women being raped, tortured, dismembered or killed.

Kim also had a file named "osu.doc" which detailed an apparent plan to rape, mutilate and strangle a girl.

Kim was out on bail when Brooke disappeared.

The Alibi

Kim said that he couldn't have been in the area of Brooke's abduction, as she was snatched between 10 and 11 a.m. on May 24. He has recorded proof that he executed a computer stock transaction at 11:14 a.m. He was also videotaped by security cameras at 12:30 p.m. buying a laptop with his father at Circuit City in Tigard.

Authorities challenged this flimsy alibi, saying not only did he have time to get from Corvallis back to Tigard in time, but that anyone could have executed that stock trade for him, as it was made from his sister's computer.

With a clear eye toward the Wilberger case, Kim was arrested on the underwear theft charges in Multnomah County, and his bail set at $10 million. Investigators in Benton, Washington and Yamhill counties, where the other colleges are located, pursued similar charges against him. Yamhill county eventually set his bail for $4 million, $1 million in Washington county, and $100,000 in Benton county.

The shadow of Brooke Wilberger hung like a shroud over his head.

The Trail Grows Cold

Family and friends of Brooke never gave up hope, never gave up the search, but as the days, weeks and months went by, momentum was hard to sustain. Cammy and Greg Wilberger, Brooke's parents, asked the media to give the family some space, some privacy.

"Our lives have been changed forever," Cammy, a teacher in the Bethel School District, said in an interview with the Register-Guard in June 2004. "Even when Brooke comes back, our lives will never be the same. The healthy thing for Brooke and ourselves is to try to be the best we can be. That includes trying to get back to some of our regular things.

"I always wondered how people could keep up hope for a long period of time," she continued. "But time fades and you don't even realize how much time has gone by. It seems like yesterday that Brooke disappeared."

The LDS church family surrounded the Wilbergers who credit their faith for sustaining them.

"We believe this life on earth is but a small part of eternity," said Marie Bell of Eugene, a former public affairs representative for the Church of Jesus Christ of Latter-Day Saints. "In the case of the Wilbergers, we believe the family is sealed together for eternity. Every fiber in my body says they will see her again."

And what kind of god could allow something like this to happen to a girl like Brooke?

Mormons, Bell said, believe God gives agency—free will—to people. "Given that, there are going to be people who use that agency in evil ways."

Cammy Wilberger said she hoped people would keep their eyes open for any clues to her daughter's whereabouts and said how touched she'd been by the considerable attention and support from friends and strangers throughout the Willamette Valley.

The reward for Brooke's safe return hit $30,000 and kept growing.

Another Blonde Coed

On November 30, 2004, a foreign exchange student in New Mexico was grabbed at knifepoint and ordered into the back of a red two-door Honda with tinted windows. The assailant drove her to a deserted parking lot and threatened to kill her unless she undressed and performed oral sex on him. He tied her ankles together with a shoelace, tied her wrists with a scarf, stuffed her panties into her mouth and pinned them there by tying another shoelace around her head.

Then he drove her to another parking lot. At one point, he stepped outside the car, and she wriggled her hands and ankles free and ran.

According to *The Oregonian*, Dana Finks, a waitress driving her three daughters to their grandmother's house in Albuquerque, was stopped at a red light when she saw a young blonde woman, wearing only an unzipped jacket with her underwear up around her neck, come running down the street. The young woman ran across traffic and into a Mexican Restaurant.

Ebony Finks, the seventeen-year-old daughter in the car, ordered her mother to pull into the restaurant parking lot, where she jumped out and met the naked girl coming out. No one inside the restaurant had offered to help her.

Hysterical, the woman got into their car and told her story in heavily accented English while Dana called 911 on her cell phone. Fresh knife marks on the woman's neck validated her story.

The red Honda drove slowly by them in the parking lot several times before the police arrived.

The victim took police to the parking lot where she was assaulted. They found a shoelace on the ground. When they interviewed neighbors, they were told that a man named Joe hung around there a lot.

With the details provided by the college student, Albuquerque police arrested Joel Patrick Courtney, a married father of three. After being treated at the hospital, the woman positively identified him as her attacker.

He was arrested and charged with first-degree criminal sexual penetration, kidnapping and aggravated battery.

A Long History of Bad Acts

Joel Patrick Courtney of Rio Rancho, New Mexico, is no stranger to the law. Just five months before being arrested for this abduction and sexual assault, his twelve-year-old son called the police on him for domestic violence against Courtney's wife. But it had started long before.

Courtney, born June 2, 1966 in Beaverton, Oregon, attended both Beaverton and Sunset High Schools. He left school in 1984. In 1985, he was charged with attempted rape and first-degree sex abuse in Oregon's Washington County.

On the night of that assault, he'd been drinking beer, smoking marijuana and snorting cocaine with a female friend from school. She was driving him home when he started to kiss and fondle her. When she pushed him away and told him to stop, he punched her, yanked her out of the car, threw her to the gravel, and pulled off her jeans and panties and unzipped his pants.

She stopped fighting, and he lost interest.

She went to the police when she found out he had done similar things in the past. They were both eighteen.

He pled guilty to first-degree sex abuse and received a three-month jail sentence and five years of probation. He subsequently violated probation and spent two and a half years in state prison.

According to Dianna Rodgers, LCSW, adjunct professor at the University of Oregon, "Rarely is an offender caught the first time he offends. Chances are, he had quite a juvenile record of assaultive behavior with some sexual component to it."

His list of infractions are lengthy, including felonies, misdemeanors and various other violations, but the one that is of the most interest is his drunk driving violation in January of 2004.

A No-Show at Court

Courtney, at the time a supervisor for a construction cleaning company, was driving a green 1997 Dodge Caravan, a company vehicle, from Portland to Newport, Oregon, to appear for his drunk driving charge on May 24, 2004, the day Brooke Wilberger disappeared. He never arrived at court.

At 1:15 p.m., he called the court and left a message that he'd been delayed, was in Corvallis, and was on his way.

According to Dr. A. Nicholas Groth, in his book *Men Who Rape—The Psychology of the Offender:* "Rape is always and foremost an aggressive act. In some offenses, the assault appears to constitute a discharge of anger; it becomes evident that the rape is the way the offender expresses and discharges a mood state of intense anger, frustration, resentment, and rage. In other offenses, the aggression seems to be reactive; that is, when the victim resists the advances of her assailant, he retaliates by striking, hitting, or hurting her in some way. Hostility appears to be quickly triggered or released, sometimes in a clear, consciously experienced stage of anger, or in other cases, in what appears to be a panic state. In still other offenses, the aggression becomes expressed less as an anger motive and more as a means of dominating, controlling, and being in charge of the situation—an expression of mastery and conquest. And in a fourth vicissitude, the aggression itself becomes eroticized so that the offender derives pleasure from both controlling his victim and hurting her/him—an intense sense of excitement and pleasure being experienced in this context whether or not actual sexual contact is made. These variations on the theme of aggression are not mutually exclusive, and, in any given instance of rape, multiple meanings may be expressed in regard to both the sexual and the aggressive behaviors."

If Courtney were particularly stressed over his upcoming court date, perhaps he had an idea of what could take the edge off that anxiety.

Groth goes on to say about those who rape in anger: "Typically, such an offender reports that he did not anticipate committing a rape. It was not something he fantasized or thought about beforehand—it was, instead, something that happened on the spur of the moment."

So that green minivan that Brian saw "driving recklessly" at or around the time of Brooke's disappearance took on a whole new meaning and a new priority level for the police.

A Routine Check

During a routine background check, Albuquerque police learned that Courtney had failed to show for his court date in Newport.

The Newport officials, upon hearing of Courtney's situation, and recalling the persistent public efforts of the Wilberger team, referred Albuquerque to the Benton County (Corvallis) police.

And there the link was made.

Sung Koo Kim was removed from investigators' list as a suspect. His relatives sued two cities, a county and nearly forty police officers for $11 million, claiming their home was searched illegally. The family was awarded $331,000. Kim was convicted in 2006 for theft and was released in 2012.

In February 2005, a judge in New Mexico granted Corvallis police a search warrant for Courtney's DNA—fingerprints, swabs of saliva and various hair from his face and pubic area.

In May, Corvallis investigators asked the public for any information about a 1997 green Dodge Caravan.

They got it.

The van was recovered, though not in New Mexico and not in Oregon. Investigators released no information about the van, fearing anything they say could compromise the case. No one wanted this case compromised.

In July, the Benton County grand jury heard testimony from thirteen live witnesses, including Wilberger's family and investigators, and reports from three experts, including two FBI crime lab analysts and a physician. FBI forensic DNA examiner Rhonda Craig who works for the FBI Laboratory in Quantico, Virginia, testified by report as did FBI DNA examiner Constance Fisher.

The grand jury returned a 19-count indictment accusing Joel Patrick Courtney, 39 years old, of 14 counts of aggravated murder, alleged in alternative theories (in other words, one count for every theory as to how he may have murdered her), two counts of aggravated kidnapping in the first degree, one count of first-degree rape, one count of first-degree sexual abuse and one count of first-degree sodomy.

In Oregon, prosecutors do not need a body to secure a guilty verdict. And, according to Benton County District Attorney Scott Heiser, his office was ready to "pursue the case aggressively. Oregon law doesn't require recovery of the body of a murder victim." He considered Courtney's arrest to be a milestone in the case, yet only a first step in what promises to be a long legal process.

The Current Status

Courtney, originally held on $100,000 cash-only bond, was held in the Bernalillo, New Mexico county jail without bond. He refused to waive extradition, which required Oregon Governor Ted Kulongoski to issue a warrant to have him delivered to Oregon for prosecution.

Courtney's sister, still living in Beaverton, has cooperated with the police. In an interview with KOIN-TV, she claims that Joel suffered a troubled childhood and has a long history of drug and alcohol problems. "If he is found guilty," she said, "he needs to be held accountable. Justice needs to be served."

New Mexico District Attorney for Bernalillo County, Kari Brandenburg, said she thinks Courtney may be linked to some other disappearances and wants investigators to examine where else Courtney may have traveled and stayed between Corvallis and Albuquerque to "see if there are any unresolved cases."

Due to restrictions on information and evidence, little is known about the green minivan—where it was found, by whom, and what investigators found inside. One can infer from the DNA reports submitted to the grand jury and their subsequent indictments, that enough evidence was found in the van to change this case from a kidnapping to a murder.

At a press conference on August 3, 2005, local investigators thanked the community for its contribution of leads to the case but said they would no longer need the public's help in terms of tips or information in the case.

Benton County District Attorney Scott Heiser would not release any information that might jeopardize what they consider to be a strong case. Heiser has never prosecuted a death penalty case and would not say whether he would seek that punishment for Courtney.

Back to Dianna Rodgers, who treated sex offenders in Lane County, Oregon for over 20 years: "Typically, violent offenders require escalating violence to satiate their escalating needs. Respites between episodes get shorter, the offenders take greater risks, and unfortunately, it is not uncommon for a sadistic rapist to eventually murder."

On August 5, Brooke's family posted a new message on the website, thanking those who helped to search for Brooke. "Our main goal remains to find Brooke and see that justice is served. We believe families are eternal and Brooke will always be a part of our family."

In a deal to avoid the death penalty, Courtney identified the place where police found Brooke's body. Courtney remains in prison, serving a life sentence without the possibility of parole.

Bibliography

America's Most Wanted.com — "Jailed man Charged with Murder"

Newsnet.byu.edu — "Man Accused in Wilberger Case"

Men Who Rape—The Psychology of the Offender by A. Nicholas Groth (Plenum Press, 1979)

The Register-Guard — "Word of Disappearance Spread Around the Globe" 5/30/04

The Register-Guard — "Hundreds Pray at Vigil" 6/1/04

The Register-Guard — "Officials to Narrow Scope" 6/5/04

The Oregonian — "Alibi Filed, Faulted on Wilberger" 6/25/04

The Register-Guard — "Women Get a Leg Up on Attackers"

7/12/04

The Oregonian — "Man Held in Panty Thefts" 9/23/04

Albuquerque Tribune — "Man Jailed in Rape Case" 12/2/04

AP Online — "A Man Once Considered A Suspect" 2/8/05

University Wire 2/18/05

KATU-TV — "Sung Koo Kim Makes an Appearance" 2/25/05

KATU News — "Documents Reveal Suspect" 8/2/05

The Register-Guard — "Man Held in Student's Death" 8/3/05

KOIN-TV — "New Mexico Man Accused" 8/3/05

The Oregonian — "A Troubling Trail" 8/4/05

Beaverton Valley Times — "Wilberger Suspect has Local Ties" 8/04/05

The New Mexican — "Background checks on New Mexico Rape Suspect" 8/4/05

The Register-Guard — "Traffic Ticket Key to Suspect's Arrest" 8/4/05

The Oregonian — "Brooke Wilberger Case Timeline" 8/04/05

Media Release: Capt. Ron Noble, City of Corvallis 8/3/05

KATU-TV — "Does Joel Courtney's DNA Link Him to Brooke?" 8/10/05

Rio Rancho Observer — "RR Man Accused of Brutal Crimes" 9/9/05

OSU Daily Barometer — "Only a Milestone" 9/9/05

Patrick Wayne Kearney and David Douglas Hill: The Trash Bag Murderers

A Teen Goes Missing

About 5:30 pm, on Sunday, March 13, 1977, John LaMay, 17, told his next-door neighbor that he was going to Redondo Beach to see a guy he'd met at a gym in downtown Los Angeles. The guy's name was Dave. When John didn't come home that night or the next day, his hysterical mother called the El Segundo police, certain that something had happened to him, claiming that her son didn't just go off for days at a time.

Police chalked it up to another teen runaway.

On March 18, John LeMay's remains were discovered beside a highway south of Corona. He had been carefully dismembered, all the body parts washed and drained of blood, and neatly packed into five industrial trash bags. Each bag was carefully sealed with nylon filament tape, and three of the bags had been crammed into an empty eighty-gallon oil drum, the other two left on the ground next to it. The boy's head was missing, but a birthmark clearly identified the remains as belonging to young, gay John LeMay.

Available Young Prey

The decade of the '70s was a confusing time for young people, particularly young gay people. The AIDS epidemic hadn't been named as a serious threat yet, gay bathhouses, gay bars and anonymous sex in parks, public toilets, and parties was at its frenzied zenith. Gays were coming out with a vengeance,

RIVERSIDE COUNTY SHERIFF
BULLETIN

OFFICIAL PUBLICATION OF SHERIFF'S DEPARTMENT, COUNTY OF RIVERSIDE, CALIFORNIA
BERNARD J. CLARK, SHERIFF

TUESDAY, JUNE 14, 1977

ARREST FOR MURDER

PATRICK WAYNE KEARNEY, WMA DOB 9-24-39
Ht. 5'10", Wt. 146 lb., Hair/Brown, Eyes/Blue

DAVID DOUGLAS HILL, WMA DOB 12-23-42
Ht. 6'2", Wt. 175 lb., Hair/Brown, Eyes/Brown

and they were finally taking what they considered their rightful freedoms.

In the wake of the "free love" sixties in San Francisco's Haight-Ashbury, young people headed to California in droves from all over more straitlaced America. Gay teens were drawn there as if to Mecca. Misunderstood youths ran away from unsympathetic parents, stuck out their thumbs and headed to their promised land.

They didn't necessarily find what they were looking for. Many of them ended up as boy prostitutes, trying to eke out a meager living. According to Dennis McDougal, in his book *Angel of Darkness*, "During the '70s and early '80s, more than a hundred young hitchhikers caught rides on the streets and freeways of southern California and didn't live to tell about it."

They were young, pretty, and eventually, desperate.

Says Berkeley Psychologist Michael Evans: "Homosexuals are an easy population to get access to in some anonymous way."

Chicago Police Sgt. Richard Sandberg put it another way: "The gays are easy prey."

The Predators at Work

Hitchhiking has never been a safe mode of transportation, but in the 1970s, getting into a car with a stranger was a horrifyingly common occurrence. Predators cruised the freeway onramps and beach highways. They frequented bars, hoping to find young boys in an agreeable state of inebriation. Sometimes they were looking for money, sometimes for quick, impersonal sex, sometimes they wanted to vent their frustrations and rage on someone, anyone, unsuspecting.

While homosexuals constitute only about 5 percent of serial killers, they are more prone to "overkill" than their straight counterparts, indulging in the more horrific extremes of torture, mutilation and dismemberment, according to Harold Schechter, in *The Serial Killer Files*. Gay men are also among the most prolific of serial killers. The sheer promiscuity of their crimes is a kind of grotesque mirror of the free-ranging sexual lifestyle embraced by so many gay men in the pre-AIDS era of the 1970s.

Why homosexual serial killers as a group should be especially sadistic is an interesting question, says Schechter, though one element is surely the prevailing homophobia of American society, which causes many gay men to grow up with a deep-seated sense of self-hatred, a violent homophobia of their own. When these feelings are combined with the psychopathology of a serial killer, the results can be particularly appalling.

The FBI estimates that somewhere between ten and fifty serial killers are still at large in America.

Patrick Kearney and David Hill

Patrick Wayne Kearney was born in Texas in 1940, the youngest of three boys. He was thin, shy, prone to illness, and an easy target for schoolyard bullies.

By the time he was eight years old, he knew he would kill people. By the time he was a much-ridiculed teen, he was actively fantasizing about murder. His fantasies were very detailed.

And then he tried it. It started in the mid-sixties in Tijuana and San Diego. He picked up guys in bars, bus stops, places where gay men congregated, looking for a quickie in the bushes. They were easy to find, easy to kill, bodies easy to dispose of in the desert.

But in his public life, Kearney appeared normal. He put his time in with the Army as well as into a short marriage. Neither of those situations suited him.

In 1962, Kearney met David Douglas Hill. Hill was married, and already an Army veteran. A 6'2" high school dropout from Lubbock, Hill joined the Army in 1960, but was quickly discharged on diagnosis of an unspecified personality disorder. Back in Lubbock, he married his high school sweetheart, and like Kearney's trial marriage, Hill's was short-lived. When he met the slightly built Kearney, Hill divorced his wife and moved to California with Kearney in 1967. Patrick got a good job as an aeronautical engineer with Hughes Aircraft, and David stayed home and kept house.

But though it was love at first sight when they met, their ten-year life together was tumultuous and stormy. Frequently, Hill would stomp out of the house and go spend a few nights with some friends. Or he'd pick up a one-night stand out of frustration and revenge. Occasionally, he went all the way home to Lubbock. But he always returned.

When Hill was gone, Kearney's impotent frustrations reached a boiling point. There was only one thing he knew that would satisfy those feelings of repressed rage.

Rage in Action

When Hill left the house after a fight, Kearney would go prowling. He'd jump in his Volkswagen and go out to pick up hitchhikers or young men from gay bars. Being of slight build, he had a surefire system of subduing his victims: he shot them in the head with a .22 caliber pistol without warning. Sometimes he'd be driving down the highway, paying strict attention to the speed limit with his left hand on the steering wheel, then shoot his victim in the passenger seat with his right.

Then he'd drive around until he found a suitably private place for him to relieve his frustrations, vent his rage, and wield his power.

As soon as he was alone with their corpses, he would undress them and have sex with them. They were pliant, uncomplaining.

And then he would employ the hacksaw and cut them into pieces. If he was at home, he did this in the bathroom, fastidiously washing each body part, draining it of blood, to keep it from smelling. He left no fingerprints in dried blood.

He learned all this from carefully reading the notorious crimes of Dean Corll, who murdered seventeen young boys in Houston, wrapped them up in trash bags, and buried them. Kearney studied Corll's heinous crimes and collected newspaper clippings as news of his torture and murder spree came to a violent conclusion when one of his vicious accomplices killed Corll with his own gun.

Most of Kearney's victims reminded him of the type of person who had given him a bad time during his teenage years: blond and arrogant. Sometimes, after he'd killed them and had sex with their corpses, he would beat them. Beat them until their faces were mush.

A Murderous Time

Patrick Kearney wasn't the only one killing young gay men in southern California during this time. The Hillside Strangler, who turned out to be Angelo Buono and his equally psychopathic cousin, Kenneth Bianchi, were plying their trade in the same area at the same time, abducting young girls, torturing them, strangling them, and dumping their bodies wherever convenient. The famed, and to-date-unidentified Zodiac killer was on the loose, taunting police and reigning terror with his random murders. The Zebra killers were randomly hacking people to death with machetes in San Francisco, and closer to home, Randy Kraft was proving to be one of the all-time most demented killers of gays, with his incomprehensible sadistic torture methods. William Bonin, with his sidekick Vernon Butts, was also committing horribly grisly murders on young gay men and discarding the remains alongside the freeways.

No wonder the police were confused. They didn't know how many serial killers they had, and they didn't know how many of them were copycat murders.

But as the body count rose, they noticed some marked differences in the *modus operandi*. One murderer, later to be identified as Randy Kraft, routinely picked up hitchhikers, or gays, or Marines, or whoever caught his fancy, drugged them, tortured his victims for hours and ended up by castrating them and shoving whatever was handy—broom handle, tree branch, pole, the victim's own genitals or underwear—into their rectum. Usually all of this while the victim was still alive and screaming.

William Bonin strangled his victims with rope, cord, or the victim's t-shirt, before raping the corpses and throwing the bodies to the side of the road.

But one killer stood out from the others by carefully dismembering his victims, cleaning them up, and tidily bagging them. The press called these the "trash bag murders." The homicide cops called them the "fag in a bag" murders.

The Psychology

Some experts claim that serial killing is an addiction. Once they begin killing (and sometimes they kill the first time by accident) serial killers find themselves addicted to murder in an intense cycle that begins with homicidal sexual fantasies that in turn spark a desperate search for crimes, leading to a brutal killing, followed by a period of cooling off and a return to normal daily routine—with all its unbearable stresses, disappointments, and hurts, which lead back to the reemerging need to start fantasizing about killing again. Once a killing cycle is triggered, it is rarely broken, according to Peter Vronsky, in *Serial Killers: the Method and Madness of Monsters*. With time, trapped in this addiction cycle, serial killers become more frenzied, and the frequency and violence of their murders escalate exponentially until they are either caught or "burn out" – the killer reaches a point where killing no longer satisfies them, and they stop of their own accord if nothing else interrupts their killing career. Some commit suicide, others move on to commit other crimes, or turn themselves in to the police.

A study of 326 U.S. male serial killers between 1800 and 1995 concluded that 87 percent had killed at least one stranger and 70 percent killed *only* strangers.

The most prolific serial killers also tend to be the most organized. They methodically stalk their victims for the best opportunity to strike so as not to be seen, and they smartly dump the bodies far away so as not to leave any clues. Although anyone can be targeted, say James Allen Fox and Jack Levin, in *The Will to Kill*, victims of serial killers tend to be the most vulnerable in society: children, prostitutes and the elderly.

But the most striking and intriguing aspect of serial murderers is the nature of their motivation: To satisfy an intense appetite for power and sadism. The serial murderer tends to kill not for love, money or revenge, but just for the fun of it—because it makes him feel good.

The Noose Tightens

Because John LaMay told his neighbor that he was going to visit someone named Dave in Redondo Beach, the police equated that name with a name that regularly appeared on the sign-in sheets at the gay bathhouses, and soon were knocking on the door of the modest Kearney/Hill home in Redondo.

Kearney and Hill welcomed them in, seemed to be relaxed, concerned about the missing boy, and totally innocent. While there, though, investigators helped themselves to a few carpet fibers, because for the first time in a trash bag murder, carpet fibers had been caught up in the nylon filament tape used to seal the bags.

The fibers matched.

As soon as the police left, Kearney destroyed all the files he'd kept on Dean Corll.

The police came back and asked for samples of both Kearney and Hill's pubic hair as well as hairs from their dog. The pair cooperated fully.

All the fibers and hair matched evidence left on LaMay's body.

But when the cops went back again, this time with a search warrant, the couple was gone.

Police found a hacksaw with a fresh, clean blade, but little bits of blood and tissue were caught up in the corners. John LaMay's blood and tissue. They found residual blood all over the bathroom, invisible to the naked eye, but clearly there under forensic examination. They found familiar nylon filament tape, and a search of Kearney's office at Hughes Aircraft offered up a source of the exact same trash bags used in what was looking like upward of twenty murders.

Public Relations as a Tool

A good public relations campaign can be hard for a criminal to outrun.

Most notably victims' families use public relations as a tool to ferret out information from the public and to keep pressure on the investigative bodies. Tearful press conferences, like those the families of Laci Peterson, Natalee Holloway and Brooke Wilberger held, keep the story in the public eye and keep the local police on their toes. Amber Alerts and America's Most Wanted television show turn citizens into amateur sleuths. Rewards, like those posted by families, tend to capture the attention of the viewing public, an outgrowth of which is a better-informed citizenry—and fewer places for a fugitive to hide.

The Hillside Strangler investigation task force was construed as a public relations vehicle. "The Los Angeles Police Department, going through the usual high-profile motions to reassure the public, set up a special task force which included the investigating officers from the Glendale Police Department and the Los Angeles Sheriff's Office. Not that they had anything new to go on, but all the busy commotion and news conferences looked good on television," according to Jan Brady, in *The Gates of Janus*.

The pressure was on Kearney and Hill, too, with their photographs displayed on posters.

The Strange Confession

When the heat was clearly on, Kearney and Hill fled to El Paso, Texas, but knew that life on the lam was not for them. The cops knew who they were, and what they looked like. At the behest of relatives, the pair returned to California, and at 1:30 p.m. on July 1, 1977, walked into Riverside County sheriff's office, pointed at a "Wanted" poster with their pictures on it and said, "We're them."

They were booked on suspicion of two murders and had been wanted for questioning in connection with six other slayings.

They were arraigned on the two murder charges and bail was set at $500,000 each.

Kearney cooperated fully with the police. He said the murders "excited him and gave him a feeling of dominance." The idea of hurting and killing someone sounded sexually exciting. When officers grilled him about picking up Marines and feeding pills and booze to his victims, they got a blank look from him. They persisted, wanting to know if he had ever put anything but his penis into his victims' rectums.

He used towels to keep the bodies from leaking all over his bathroom before he dismembered them, Kearney told them. The police persisted, hoping to put to rest more of their freeway mysteries. How about torture? Did he ram anything into an anus for the sheer pleasure of it? Recognition crossed Kearney's face and he shook his head. "I am *not* the Wooden Stake," he said. He knew exactly what the detectives were getting at, but impaling, strangling and torturing his victims wasn't his style. A bullet to the head was clean and simple.

He seemed offended that he would be confused with Randy Kraft.

Horrific Details

The Trash Bag Murders investigation began officially on April 13, 1975, when the body of Albert Rivera, 21, of Los Angeles, was found near Highway 74, east of San Juan Capistrano, in a heavy-duty trash bag.

But according to Kearney, in a series of letters, confessions and conversations with the police, the killing began much earlier. In the mid 60s in Tijuana and San Diego.

He led them to the site where he had buried one of his first victims, known only as George, behind his and Hill's Culver City apartment, killed around Christmas, 1968. The police dug where Kearney indicated, and came up with a skeleton with a single bullet hole in its skull.

After killing George, a paranoid Kearney laid low for over a year. Nobody came knocking on his door, and he realized that he had actually gotten away with murder.

A neighbor said she occasionally heard what she thought were gunshots but had no idea they came from the Kearney and Hill apartment.

After his arrest, Kearney wrote letters to the police, detailing the crimes, the names of the victims and the places the bodies could be found. An 18th count of murder was filed the same day that the 13th Hillside Strangler victim was found.

As to John LaMay? Hill wasn't home when his young lover came to the house, so Kearney invited him in to watch television. Without provocation, Kearney shot LaMay in the back of the head, and later dumped his remains in the desert. He liked using the desert. The desert animals and insects removed evidence quickly and efficiently. "Things disappear very rapidly in the desert," he told investigators. "You can put a small animal on an anthill, and it disappears right in front of your eyes."

A Few Close Calls

According to Dennis McDougal, Kearney once had a flat tire during one of his drives to the desert to dispose of a body. When he discovered that the spare was flat, too, he had to call a tow truck to get his car to a service station. Kearney stood by, sweating bullets while the attendant fixed the flat, never questioning the bags in the back seat, which contained arms, legs, a rib cage and some intestines.

Another time he locked his keys in the car while inspecting possible dump sites. It took him hours to jimmy open the lock with a coat hanger, nervously looking over his shoulder the whole time, freshly filled trash bags again in the back seat.

As soon as the bags were unloaded, though, he felt an enormous sense of relief, accomplishment, and power.

A Surprise Twist

While Kearney was happy to discuss his activities, after hearing three hours of evidence, the Riverside County Grand Jury refused to indict David Hill.

Public Defender Malcolm MacMillan spirited him out of jail under a cloak of secrecy to protect him from reporters and photographers. Hill fled California and returned to Lubbock.

Riverside District Attorney Byron Morton said, "the evidence against Mr. Hill was weak," adding that much of the information unearthed by Riverside investigators tended to exonerate Hill. McMillan said he was not surprised the grand jury refused to indict Hill, adding that he did not think there was sufficient evidence to hold him to answer in Superior Court.

Kearney said that Hill was neither involved in nor aware of the murders. He said that he committed all the murders while Hill was away.

Did Kearney take all the blame to free an innocent man, or to absolve his lover? Is it likely that Hill was innocent?

The Plea, The Sentence

Against the advice of his attorney, Patrick Kearney changed his not guilty plea to a plea of guilty. His attorney advised him to plead Not Guilty by Reason of Insanity, but Kearney pled guilty to the original three charges of murder and asked to be sentenced immediately. This was an apparent move to avoid California's death penalty. His actions were moot; the death penalty law didn't go into effect until August, 1977. All Kearney's homicides predated that time, so the death penalty was never an option for prosecutors.

Superior Judge John Hews handed down a life term with the possibility of parole in seven years.

Judge Breckenridge said "This defendant has certainly

perpetrated a series of ghastly and grisly crimes. I can only hope the community release board will never release Mr. Kearney. He appears to be an insult to humanity."

For what seems to be approximately thirty-two murders, Kearney was eventually charged with 21 counts of murder and received 21 life sentences.

If all of his confessions are truthful, he also murdered two children, ages 5 and 8, along with four victims whose bodies were never recovered. At least seven of his victims remain unidentified.

The Status

Patrick Kearney is today living out his life sentences in California. He writes essays and has had a few of them published.

David Hill played himself in an episode of "History's Mysteries: Infamous Murders" for the History Channel in 2001.

The Trash Bag Murders are considered among the most heinous crimes of the twentieth century. Patrick Kearney's swath of death ranks him with the likes of Jerry Brudos, Ted Bundy, Jeffrey Dahmer and John Wayne Gacy.

According to Los Angeles Homicide Sergeant Al Sett, "If he hadn't gotten sloppy, consciously or unconsciously, he'd probably still be doing it today."

Bibliography

Peter Vronsky, *Serial Killers: The Method and Madness of Monsters* (Berkley Books, 2004)

James Alan Fox, & Jack Levin, *The Will to Kill* (Allyn & Bacon Books, 2001)

Dennis McDougal, *Angel of Darkness*, (Warner Books 1991)

IDMb.com "History's Mysteries: Notorious Murders"

Jan Brady, *The Gates of Janus*, (Los Angeles: Feral House, 2001)

Public Relations Quarterly: Serial Murder Public Relations Tactics, 2004

Time Magazine, July 18, 1977 — "Twenty-eight and Counting"

Time Magazine, July 12, 1993 — "The Landscaper's Secrets"

The Los Angeles Times, July 2, 1977 — "Suspects in Eight Slayings Surrender"

The Los Angeles Times, July 3, 1977 — "Two Suspects May Be Connected to 43 Murders"

The Los Angeles Times, July 4, 1977 — "Evidence Near Body Reportedly Led to Suspects"

The Los Angeles Times, July 6, 1977 — "Pair Arraigned in 2 'Trash Bag' Murder Cases"

The Los Angeles Times, July 8, 1977 — "Skeleton Dug Up"

The Los Angeles Times, July 15, 1977 — "One Man Indicted"

The Los Angeles Times, December 22, 1977 — "Admitted Killer of 15 Men, Boys"

The Los Angeles Times, December 23, 1977 — "Man Sentenced in 'Trash Bag Murders'"

The Los Angeles Times, January 7, 1978 — "Confessed Trash Bag Killer Quizzed"

The Los Angeles Times, January 10, 1978 — "'Trash Bag' Slayer Names 4 Victims"

The Los Angeles Times, February 16, 1978 — "'Trash Bag Killer' Faces 17 More Counts"

The Los Angeles Times, February 18, 1978 — "Apparent 13th Slaying by Hillside Killer"

The Los Angeles Times, February 18, 1978 — "18th 'Trash Bag'

Murder Count Filed"

The Los Angeles Times, February 22, 1978 — "'Trash Bag' Slayer Pleads Guilty"

Russell Obremski: A Killer's Luck

The Rampage

In the early afternoon of Monday, February 3, 1969 in the small town of Medford, Oregon, neighbors of LaVerna Mae and Clifford Lowe heard shouting. Then they heard screaming—lots of it—but they couldn't tell where it was coming from. A short time later, they heard shots fired. Four of them.

At three o'clock, LaVerna's eight-year-old daughter Becky came home from school to find her mother, eight months pregnant, wearing only her robe and a torn bra, dead in a pool of blood on the sofa, four bullet holes in her head.

At 3:30 p.m. that same day, sixteen-year old William Ritchie and his brother, eleven-year old Robert, left their widowed mother in her car in the parking lot of the pharmacy while they ran inside to pick up her prescription. Ten minutes later, they came out of the store to find her car missing.

A few parking spots away, a hay truck idled, abandoned.

The following day, Betty Ann Ritchie's nude body was discovered on Carberry Creek Road, thirty-four miles southwest of Medford. She'd been killed by a single .22 shot to the temple, the muzzle of the gun held tightly against her head.

Twenty-four-year-old Russell Obremski was on a spree.

His was a case that continued to terrorize the citizens of Oregon and confound the legal system for twenty-five more years.

A Long History of Violence

Russell Loren Obremski was born in 1945 in Fort Klamath, Oregon. His mother died when Russell was 10, and he continued to live with his stepfather, who Obremski claimed drank a lot and beat him with regularity. A year later, he moved to Klamath Falls and was adopted by his grandparents.

Russell's entire history reads like that of a troubled man. He progressed from minor difficulties as a teen to larger difficulties as a man. According to family physician Dr. Neal Black, Russell was unable to adjust to life without his mother. He lied frequently, had poor grades, was retained in fifth grade, and passed from seventh to eighth only because of his age. Russell always had difficulty with other children, both in the classroom and out of the school.

In school counseling sessions, his grandmother always tried to overprotect him and blame his problems on someone else.

Eventually, his disciplinary and truancy problems became so overwhelming, and he was so disruptive, that he was excused from Henley High School and asked not to return.

Obremski was subject to violent outbursts. His juvenile record began at age twelve and included breaking school windows, making lewd phone calls, threatening girls with a knife, vandalism, and stealing gasoline.

He spent time at MacLaren School for boys, a juvenile detention center in Woodburn, Oregon, just south of Portland. Two months after being released from MacLaren, he beat up a younger, smaller boy on the street for no apparent reason.

He'd been sniffing glue.

When he threatened his grandmother, she had him committed to the state hospital for a year. She was convinced his violent outbursts were the result of a type of epilepsy.

Before the Medford murders, Obremski served time for adult offenses including larceny, vagrancy, and escaping from a correctional institution. His most serious conviction, however, was for carnal knowledge, which involved intercourse with a fourteen-year-old girl.

He was released from a penitentiary a mere five months before that horrendous February day in Medford.

He'd been sentenced to twenty years.

He served only fourteen months.

A Killing Spree

February 1, 1969 was a cold Saturday morning. Russell Obremski jumped into a truck loaded with hay along with Don Slaughter, 26, in his hometown of Klamath Falls, Oregon. They were headed seventy miles away for White City, Oregon to deliver the hay. Slaughter had arranged for them to deliver the hay and then stay at the home of Clifford Lowe, a friend in Medford, for a couple of nights before returning to Klamath.

While they were traveling down Dead Indian Road, a .22 caliber handgun on a shelf above the driver's seat fell down, landed on the seat and discharged, hitting Slaughter in the right leg. Obremski took over the driving, and drove Slaughter to Providence Hospital, where he stayed for four days.

Obremski continued to White City, unloaded the hay, then went to the home of Clifford Lowe, as had been arranged. Lowe and Obremski had known each other for a few years when they were younger, but were not close friends, and had had little contact over the years.

Lowe generously opened his home to Obremski to stay for a couple of nights with his family, which included his pregnant wife and their five children.

The next day, Sunday, Obremski used the hay truck to deliver a load of auto parts to Ashland, and in the process, Cliff Lowe happened to see the handgun.

On Monday, Clifford Lowe had to go to work. Their five children, ranging in age from fifteen to eight years old were going to school, and Cliff was having a hard time leaving the house, knowing his eight-months-pregnant wife would then be alone with the six-foot one inch, two-hundred-pound Obremski.

Despite his misgivings, his wife assured him she would be

fine.

Cliff should have paid attention to that inner voice.

The Day Turns Deadly

At 3:30 that afternoon, he came home to find police at his house and his murdered wife inside on the couch.

They'd been married less than a year.

About the time Cliff Lowe was arriving home, Obremski, his brain clouded from inhaling model airplane glue fumes, had already kidnapped Betty Ritchie, and was driving her car out of the pharmacy parking lot. He headed south, along back roads.

Traffic on rural Carberry Creek Road is intermittent. Everybody knows everybody else, what cars they drive, and usually, what their business is. Witnesses in that backwoods area between just north of the California border saw a red '67 Impala go down Carberry Creek Road with two people in it, and a short while later, saw the car come back with only one man driving.

When the news bulletins hit describing Obremski, Mrs. Ritchie and the car, calls came into the local sheriff's office.

It wasn't long afterward that Mrs. Ritchie's body was found. According to the Medford Mail Tribune, Obremski would later say that he forced Mrs. Ritchie to undress in an attempt to delay her reporting the theft of her car, but when she became hysterical, he lost patience and shot her in the face, threw her down an embankment, tossed her clothes after her, and went to buy some beer.

He stopped at the Copper Store for his six-pack. When asked by the clerk if he didn't just go by with a woman in his car, he got a little testy and said that he was giving a relative, Betty Rodriguez, a ride home from Klamath. But both Obremski and the store clerk knew that wasn't true. No Betty Rodriguez lived up Carberry Creek Road.

The next tip for police, as the manhunt continued, came the following day from Santa Cruz, California. Two surfers were offered a ride by Obremski. They saw his gun on the front seat of the red Impala, saw the blood all over the back seat, declined the ride, and called the police.

Russell Obremski, never known for being bright, was easy to find. California police identified the red car, stopped it, and knowing that the suspect was armed, approached the vehicle with shotguns drawn.

Obremski gave himself up without incident.

Arrested

Once in jail, though, Obremski refused to waive extradition to be sent back to Oregon where he was well known in the penal system, and where the bodies of his victims awaited justice. Santa Cruz convened a grand jury, which heard twenty witnesses testify. Extradition papers were signed without delay by Governor Ronald Reagan, and Obremski was shipped to the Jackson County Jail. He was arraigned on March 11 in the Medford court of Judge L.L. Sawyer.

He was assigned Public Defenders Patrick Ford and Carl M. Brophy, who entered pleas of innocent by reason of insanity. Obremski was held without bail.

In an interview with *48 Hours*, Obremski said that at that point, he wanted to die. He deserved the death penalty.

He deserved to die.

The Trial

There was little doubt about who killed LaVerna Mae Lowe and Betty Ann Ritchie. In spite of a failed motion by the defense attorneys for a change of venue, the trial opened in Medford on September 9, 1969.

According to testimony, at 1:30 p.m. on the day of the murders, Don Slaughter called Mrs. Lowe and told her he didn't want Obremski to drive the hay truck.

An hour later, Slaughter saw Obremski drive the truck past his hospital room window toward the shopping center, where Mrs. Ritchie had her prescriptions filled. He also identified the murder weapon, a .22 handgun, as his own, which he kept in the hay truck; it was the same gun that had wounded him in the leg as they drove down from Klamath Falls.

The neighbor who had heard screaming testified that she saw a man drive a green hay truck away from the Lowes' house that afternoon.

The coroner testified that sperm was found during the autopsies. Whether it was found in the widow Betty Ritchie or eight-month-pregnant LaVerna Lowe was not clear. There was no evidence of "sexual assault," i.e. trauma, to either woman, and in those days of pre-DNA evidence, sexual assault or rape charges were never filed.

While Obremski did not testify at this trial, in later interviews, he claimed that he does not remember killing either woman, he claims to not even remember kidnapping Betty Ritchie, but he vehemently denies committing sexual assault on either of them.

Obremski remembers a lot about his crimes, for having no memory of them.

The Prosecution

The most damaging witness was repairing fences along Carberry Creek Road. He saw the red car with a man and a woman in it go by. Later, the man alone in the car stopped at the Copper Store. When the witness asked the defendant where the woman was, he was told he'd taken her home, about five miles up Carberry Creek Road. In an effort to identify the woman who lived five miles up Carberry Creek Road, the witness asked what her husband did, and an annoyed Obremski responded, "John. You know John." Obremski bought a six-pack of beer and left. The witness then called the police, and the two of them drove up Carberry Creek Road together, looking for tire tracks in the snow. They found them, and then they found the nude body of Mrs. Ritchie, who had been dumped out. Her body had slid twenty-five feet down the snowy embankment. Her clothes were strewn about the area.

Police testified that Mrs. Ritchie's nylon stockings were found in the back seat of her car, glued together. Several tubes of model airplane glue were found on the floor of the hay truck as well as in the red Impala.

Cellmates testified that Obremski told them he'd made a pass at Mrs. Lowe who had slapped him. Then he dragged her into the bedroom. When asked what he did then, he said, "What do you think I done? Bam! Bam! I'd do it again."

After calling 63 witnesses, the prosecution rested.

There was no doubt that Obremski committed the murders. But his plea was "innocent by reason of insanity."

Was Obremski legally insane?

The Defense

The defense had been fairly quiet during the state's presentation of the evidence. Defense attorneys rarely challenged witnesses and many times did not even cross-examine them. Clearly, their entire defense rested on the insanity plea.

The first day of the defense, Obremski appeared for the first time wearing handcuffs chained to his waist. Earlier that morning, jail attendants investigating a noise found a hacksaw blade hidden in his mattress. He'd been sawing the bars of his cell. In a violent outburst at being caught, Obremski kicked in the toilet, tore out pipes and damaged the washbasin, sending water gushing down an electrical conduit passage into courthouse offices below. He had threatened to stick one of his defense attorneys in the eye with a pencil and tried to hit the other one with a chair. The attorneys asked the judge to order him chained.

A Psychopath

The defense attorney's first move was to call Dr. Neal Black, the defendant's family doctor, who called Obremski a "constitutional psychopath." According to Dr. Black, Obremski was the type of person who acted on the spur of the moment and would not give much consideration to what he was about to do. Such an individual doesn't obey the rules of society, but Dr. Black would not go so far as to say that Obremski did not know right from wrong.

Dr. James G. Shanklin, a Portland psychiatrist who had studied Obremski's file, but had never interviewed him in person, said that the facts presented were characteristic of a mentally ill person, said illness apparently being of lifelong duration. Obremski's case history would suggest a person suffering from schizophrenia, with an element of paranoia. That disease would affect his emotions, intelligence, and social relations, the doctor testified. It would cause a withdrawal from reality, unusual sensitivity to attraction or rejection, love or hate, and such a person would engage in a good deal of fantasy. Someone with those symptoms would have great resistance to emotional stress. He could be sensitive, possibly withdrawn, or might turn about suddenly and become extremely aggressive.

"His tolerance to pressure would be low," Dr. Shanklin testified. Would he know the consequences of his actions? "There is nothing in his case history to suggest this man ever deliberated in his life. Mentally ill and intoxicated, he was incapable of deliberating, plotting, and carrying through any organized scheme. I don't think he was able to distinguish between right and wrong." And yet, had the psychiatrist ever examined Obremski? No, he had not. He was speaking hypothetically.

Dr. Richard Lahti testified that in his opinion Obremski had suffered brain damage from his mother's being in labor with his birth for fifty-six hours, and his history of glue sniffing.

Obremski did not testify.

The Verdict

After deliberating for nine hours and thirty-five minutes over two days, the jury reached a unanimous verdict: guilty on two counts of first-degree murder. According to one juror who was subsequently interviewed by the *Eugene Register Guard*, the whole insanity plea was rejected in the first few minutes of their deliberations.

In Oregon, first-degree murder carried a mandatory life sentence, with automatic appeals.

"This is a man who should never be out of jail," Justin Smith, Jackson County District Attorney, told *48 Hours*.

At sentencing, Judge Sawyer was not specific as to whether Obremski's life sentences would be served concurrently or consecutively. "The question of whether the sentences be served consecutively or concurrently is moot," Judge Sawyer said. "For this reason, the court will remain silent, but I feel sure that Mr. Obremski will not be released to return to society and should not be released upon society."

This is a statement Judge Sawyer would live to regret.

A Killer Walks Free

Obremski would be eligible for parole in ten years if the sentences ran concurrently, or in twenty years if they ran consecutively. If Obremski had served his terms consecutively, he would be eligible for parole in 1989.

In 1977, the Matrix system was implemented as a parole tool in the state of Oregon. Designed to reduce prison overcrowding, the matrix system is a complicated formula that sets a definite release date for all prisoners. For Obremski, the parole board calculated a November 1986 release date. This means Obremski would serve a mere seventeen years for committing two heinous murders.

In 1986, a Victim's Rights law was passed, allowing victims' families to speak at parole hearings. At every one of Obremski's parole hearings, his victims' families were there to speak. Especially vocal was Pam Nelson, LaVerna Lowe's daughter. She was there to fight. She circulated petitions throughout Oregon. "My goal was to keep him in prison, where he belongs," she told *48 Hours*.

Ultimately, her efforts, while successful in bringing attention to this case and affecting change in the parole system, didn't keep Obremski behind bars.

Obremski's parole date was extended five times, finally to November 8, 1993.

When he passed a psychological exam, the parole board lost its ability to keep him in prison. Dr. Robert Davis, the psychiatrist that the parole board hired to evaluate Obremski, said, "I concluded that Mr. Obremski was not a clear and present danger."

Obviously, the parole board took major criticism for releasing him, suggesting that the board could have shopped around for another psychological recommendation that would have found Obremski unfit for release.

Obremski's prison record was not taken into account when his parole was granted, despite a list of infractions, which included possession of narcotics, undetailed sexual activity, disobedience, and false statements to the staff.

In spite of over 50,000 petition signatures asking to keep him in prison, on November 8, 1993, Russell Obremski was paroled.

Public Outcry

The National Rifle Association and gubernatorial candidate Denny Smith weighed in, seeking reform and pointing fingers.

The last of LaVerna Lowe's children, who had remained in Oregon, moved out of state They were afraid for their lives after having been so vocally adamant about Obremski never again seeing the light of day.

The CBS program *48 Hours* was there to document his first free steps after almost twenty-five years in prison.

Public outcry was intense. Danny Santos, former chairman of the parole board, was at the center of the firestorm. Gubernatorial candidate Denny Smith turned it and the three-strikes-and-you're-out initiative into his major campaign issue.

The NRA placed full-page ads in all the local newspapers, demanding reform. In fact, sixteen states have now abolished parole entirely, requiring convicts to serve their entire sentences.

In March 1994, the Oregon parole board made major

policy renovations, implementing a panel of two to three psychologists (instead of just one) for murderers, the most serious sex offenders, and inmates convicted under Oregon's dangerous offender statutes. The psychological examinations are now part of an overall evaluation package, not the sole determining factor in setting a release date.

In 1994, the federal government passed a crime bill, which provides financial incentives to states that enact a Truth in Sentencing statute, i.e., requiring prisoners to serve at least 85% of their sentences before being considered for parole. Representative Elizabeth Furst of Oregon invoked Obremski's heinous crimes to help persuade the U.S. legislature to pass this crime bill.

Obremski's sister, his only staunch and steadfast supporter said, in an interview with *48 Hours*, "He was tried and convicted. Is it fair to retry him all the time?"

Conditions of his parole included checking in with his parole officer once a week for three years, no alcohol consumption, not leaving the state without permission, not owning or possessing any weapons or controlled substances.

He went to live in a halfway house in Eugene, Oregon, got a job feeding livestock on a ranch, found himself a girlfriend and a dog, went to AA meetings, did a little fishing, went to counseling sessions, and took Antabuse, a drug that makes a person violently ill if they drink any alcohol while taking it.

Obremski's parole officer Al McCann gave Obremski a fifty-fifty chance of making it. Sentencing Judge Lawrence Sawyer said, "There's no way to rehabilitate a man like him. He's a sociopath."

Just One Beer

Over Valentine's Day weekend in 1994, Obremski took his girlfriend to a motel in the coastal town of Florence, Oregon and proposed marriage. He stopped taking the Antabuse just in case she accepted his proposal. When she said yes, he went across the street and bought two bottles of beer, and they toasted their good fortune and rosy future.

The beer made him violently ill. He was sick in the bathroom all night long, thanks to the residual Antabuse still in his system.

At the next meeting with his parole officer, Obremski admitted his alcohol consumption, a parole violation. The general punishment for such a violation is a 27-day jail sentence in the nearest county facility.

But "drinking for one type of offender might not be as serious an offense as it would be for another," parole board member Diane Middle said. Both Medford victims were murdered while Obremski was on a drug and alcohol binge.

This, then, was a more serious infraction than Russell had expected.

The episode of *48 Hours* aired on March 9.

Obremski was fired from his job immediately afterward.

The Horrific Inevitable

While everyone anticipated another incident, another arrest, another trial, another sentence, nobody expected what happened next. March 18, 1994, just four months after being paroled, Russell Obremski was arrested again. This time it was for first-degree sexual abuse and first-degree sodomy against a four-year-old girl. The child was a relative of his fiancée's.

I-told-you-so's were rampant in the media and among those in the penal and parole systems. Obremski said he'd been set up by his fiancée's relatives to keep her from marrying him.

With all the media hype, Obremski considered himself a political prisoner.

Judge Sawyer, who originally sentenced Obremski after his murder trial, told a *48 Hours* update that the only thing that surprised him about the new allegations was the age of the victim.

Oregon was again horrified. The citizens, the media, LaVerna Lowe's children, Betty Ritchie's boys, all were on the edge of their seats.

After his arrest, Obremski was denied bail.

Not because of his history, nor because of the severity of this crime. No, he was denied bail because he had committed a parole violation. He drank half of a beer on Valentine's Day.

Another Trial

From the beginning, Obremski denied the molestation charge. He had been babysitting the four-year-old relative of his fiancée. He took her and her nine-year-old friend to Armitage Park, where the accused said he took her across a footbridge to a fallen log where she said Obremski licked her genitals and showed her his "tail with whiskers around it."

The trial began September 29, 1994 and included twelve days of testimony, which included Obremski slamming his fist on the stand, vehemently denying everything. His testimony was confusing, and he contradicted himself several times. Eventually, he said he remembered telling the girl to behave, or he'd "hit her a good lick on the butt." This is where he says she got the idea to tell her friend, her mother, two investigators and a counselor, "Uncle Russ licked my butt."

The young accuser was not allowed to testify.

The jury deliberated 7 hours over two days before voting to acquit. There was just not enough evidence. Several of the jurors felt that the charges were trumped up, trying to get him back into prison.

According to one juror, "We wanted to put him back in prison or fry for his first crimes, but we weren't there to try him for that."

Lane County District Attorney Doug Harcleroad agreed that not having the young accuser testify, even on videotape, was what sounded the death knell for the prosecution's case. The jurors just did not know how credible the young witness was.

Though acquitted of the molestation charges, Obremski remained in jail on the parole violation charge.

Aftermath

Russell Obremski remained in the Oregon State Penitentiary, having had his parole permanently revoked on the violations charge of drinking a beer to celebrate his engagement. "Getting the rest of my life in prison is what I get for being honest, for keeping my word to my parole officer," Obremski told reporters. "I gave him my word that I would never lie to him, and I didn't. And it was Olde English 800. If I'd known they were going to do this, hell, I would have bought Budweiser."

His fiancée stuck by him.

"I'm a nice guy," Obremski told journalists.

Russell Obremski's unusual case provided grounds for many prison and sentencing reforms, but the Matrix System is still used in Oregon to compute parole dates for violent crimes committed before 1989.

In 2005, Obremski died in prison at the age of 60.

Bibliography

Medford Mail Tribune — "Klamath Falls Man Sought" February 4, 1969

Medford Mail Tribune — "Extradition is Under Way" February 4, 1969

Medford Mail Tribune — "Two Indictments Are Returned" February 12, 1969

Medford Mail Tribune — "Obremski Hearing Set for Monday" March 7, 1969

Medford Mail Tribune — "Obremski Arraigned" March 11, 1969

Medford Mail Tribune — "Psychiatrists" August 8, 1969

Medford Mail Tribune — "Change of Venue" August 22, 1969

Medford Mail Tribune — "Change of Venue Denied" September 3, 1969

Medford Mail Tribune — "Testimony Opens" September 15, 1969

Medford Mail Tribune — "No Sign of Assault" September 16, 1969

Medford Mail Tribune — "State Has Called 40 Witnesses" September 17, 1969

Medford Mail Tribune — "Testimony Centers on Blood Stains" September 18, 1969

Medford Mail Tribune — "Ex-Inmates Testify" September 19, 1969

Medford Mail Tribune — "Obremski Called 'Psychopath'" September 22, 1969

Medford Mail Tribune — "Defense Witnesses Continue" September 23, 1969

Medford Mail Tribune — "Psychiatrists Due" September 24, 1969

Medford Mail Tribune — "Defense Rests" September 25, 1969

Medford Mail Tribune — "Unanimous Jury Verdict" September 30, 1969

Medford Mail Tribune — "Obremski Gets Two Life Terms" October 7, 1969

CBS News *48 Hours* — "A Killer Walks Free" March 9, 1994

Eugene Register Guard — "48 Hours Stirs Old Issues" March 11, 1994

Eugene Register Guard — "Obremski's Arrest Stirs Reaction" March 18, 1994

Eugene Register Guard — "Parolee Held in Sex Abuse Case"

March 20, 1994

CBS News *48 Hours* — "Love in Black & White" March 23, 1994

Eugene Register Guard — "Obremski Enters No Guilty Plea" March 25, 1994

Eugene Register Guard — "Judge Sets high bail" March 29, 1994

Eugene Register Guard — "Obremski Parole Draws More Fire" April 6, 1994

Eugene Register Guard — "Parole Policy will be Revised" April 21, 1994

Eugene Register Guard — "Trial to Start" August 25, 1994

Eugene Register Guard — "Obremski Denies Abusing Girl" October 1, 1994

Eugene Register Guard — "Sides Sum Up" October 5, 1994

Eugene Register Guard — "Jury finds Obremski Not Guilty" October 7, 1994

Eugene Register Guard — "Board Revokes Killer's Parole" October 19, 1994

Eugene Register Guard — "Parole Board Slams Door" December 8, 1994

Eugene Register Guard — "Killer Says Politics Did Him In" December 11, 1994

CBS News *48 Hours* — "A Killer Walks Free Update" August 10, 1998

"Trends in Probation and Parole in the States" by William D. Burrell

"Truth in Sentencing in State Prisons" Bureau of Justice Statistics, January 1999

Robert Spangler:

Divorce by Grand Canyon

A Sudden Tragedy

When Timothy Trevithick received no answer to his knock on Susan Spangler's front door about 10:30 in the morning on December 30, 1978, he thought that was odd. Susan, his fifteen-year-old girlfriend, was inside. He knew her brother and mother were both at home, too. Perhaps they had all overslept.

He knocked harder. And again, more insistently.

No answer.

Finally, Tim went around the house to the back, but found all the doors locked. He eventually shimmied through a basement window and went up the stairs, to find Susan apparently asleep in her bed.

Upon closer examination, he saw she was dead. She'd been shot, once, in the back. Her brother, David, was dead in his bed, too, after an apparent struggle. David had died with his head and shoulders on the floor, his feet still up on the bed. Blood from a single gunshot stained the front of his shirt.

Tim called the police.

When Susan's father Bob came home later that day from the movies, he found police cars and ambulances at his Littleton, Colorado home.

Inside was the ultimate horror: Not only were his children dead in their beds, but police found Nancy, his wife of 23 years, slumped over in her chair near the typewriter where she had written her suicide note, Bob's Smith and Wesson .38 revolver

on the floor by her. Upstairs, in their bedroom, a stepstool was still in front of the closet where he kept his gun in the back of the top shelf.

They'd been having marital troubles, Bob told the police, but he had no idea that Nancy was capable of anything like this. They'd been separated for nine months, but he had recently moved back into the house and they were trying their best to reconcile.

He agreed to take a polygraph test, to cooperate in any way that he could.

His hands and gloves were tested for gunshot residue, and then the technician who tested him for the telltale gunshot powder, took the distraught Spangler home with him for a spaghetti dinner and to spend the night with his family. They were old friends.

And so, in one fell swoop, Robert Spangler was free of all family encumbrances. To all outward appearances, the event devastated him, but those who knew Nancy suspected there was more to the story.

They were right.

High School Sweethearts

Robert Spangler and Nancy Stahlman started dating in junior high school in their hometown of Ames, Iowa. According to Robert Scott in his book *Married to Murder*, Bob was a high school football hero, and Nancy was the All-American girl involved in a wide variety of extra-curricular activities. They looked like they belonged together. Nancy certainly thought so.

Bob was born in Des Moines, Iowa on January 10, 1933. He was adopted by Merlin and Ione Spangler of Ames, Iowa. Merlin was a professor and researcher at Iowa State University. A brilliant scholar, Merlin wrote a textbook, served in as an officer in both World wars, and helped formulate the Marsten/Spangler theory of soil pressure on underground conduits, which survives to this day. There is even a geo-technical laboratory on the ISU campus named for him.

Bob, not having the benefit of the genetic makeup of his adopted father, had only his good looks and athletic aptitude to lean on. And a gift for acting. He went to college at his father's school, Iowa State, more because it was expected of him than his interest in higher education, but he finished with a degree in technical journalism, and Nancy was there, too, a member of the synchronized swimming team and the yearbook staff.

They were married in 1955, and after a stint in the Army, Bob and Nancy settled down to raise a family and make a good home. Friends said she'd never been happier. Bob went to work for American Waterworks, moved them to Littleton, Colorado, not far from Denver, and in 1961, son David was born, followed in 1963 by daughter Susan. Nancy discovered a passion for gourmet cooking, and the family, to all outward appearances, was a perfect one.

Nancy's family's suspicions

The first thing that got the Stahlman family suspicious about the murders was their conviction that their Nancy would never hurt herself or her children. Her children were her life, according to the *Denver Rocky Mountain News*. Nancy's friends and family members knew that she and Bob had been having some marital difficulties—he even moved out for a time, but the day before the murders, she was upbeat and hopeful about their reconciliation, in spite of the fact that Bob had been having an affair with a coworker.

And then there were the inconsistencies in Spangler's story and the evidence.

Shortly after the murders, Spangler's story changed. Later, he told police that he came home, saw the bodies, and then went to the movies, without calling anybody. He said he meant to call the police, and he was going to when he got back home again, after he'd had a chance to process what he'd seen, but by the time he got back home, the police were already there, having been summoned by Susan's boyfriend.

There were more inconsistencies.

The tests showed gunshot residue on Bob's gloves but not on Nancy's hand.

Tests showed no fingerprints on the typewriter, but instead, there were obvious "wipe marks." Why would Nancy wipe the keys of her typewriter after typing a suicide note that she had merely signed with her initial "N"?

Then the coroner determined that the handgun was fired from "intermediate range," meaning two to eight inches away from her head. Most self-inflicted gunshot wounds are contact wounds, the muzzle of the gun pressing against the skin. Women hardly ever shoot themselves in the face, but Nancy's bullet entry wound was high on her forehead. She had a neurological disorder that resulted in weakness and unsteadiness in her hands, casting further suspicions on whether or not she could hold a gun so far from her forehead and fire it.

Besides, Nancy was afraid of guns.

Not only was it unlikely she could or would fire a gun like that at herself, there was no way she could have wrestled with seventeen-year-old David, who clearly had wrestled with someone. Nancy weighed about a hundred pounds.

And then the gun was found five and a half feet away from her body.

None of this added up to Nancy's relatives. Even the police were suspicious, but there was no concrete evidence with which to charge her husband, Bob Spangler.

He even showed up for his polygraph test. Twice. Both times he hyperventilated, rendering the tests useless.

He was nervous, he said.

Her family said he knew how to ace the test.

He had all three bodies cremated right away.

The Lonely Widower

Bob Spangler was at his best with a woman by his side to admire his athletic abilities, and on July 14, 1979, just seven months after the death of his entire family, and at the age of

46, he again married, and his new wife moved into the home he had once shared with Nancy and the kids.

Sharon Cooper was a fit hiker and a writer; whose passion was the Grand Canyon. She was sparkly and bubbly (although she suffered from manic depression and took a cocktail of drugs in an attempt to control that dark side of her personality), and Bob had been enamored of her ever since they met as coworkers at American Water Works. In fact, they had become lovers not long after they met, but they kept their affair under wraps. The fact that Bob had been married for 23 years and would likely lose half or more of everything should Nancy divorce him, was a great incentive for discretion.

Still, their neighbors—all friends of Nancy's—were aghast that Bob would replace her and the children as quickly as he did, but he paid no attention to them. He was off on a new adventure; the whole chapter of family life with children had been closed. Bob readily admitted that he had a talent for compartmentalizing things, and that he didn't care to live in the past. His new life consisted of Sharon, hikes in the Grand Canyon, and her three dogs, which were better than children. They didn't talk back, they didn't smoke dope, they respected him and behaved as they ought to. Sharon was a strict disciplinarian with the dogs Sunshine, Shadow, and Mollie, and they were perfectly trained.

In 1986, two things of importance happened in the Spangler household. The first was that Sharon's book, *One Foot in the Grand Canyon* was published to good reviews and earned her a reputation as an authentic, realistic hiker and nature writer who laid it on the line with regards to the danger as well as the beauty of many of the Grand Canyon trails. She didn't sugar coat anything.

The other thing that happened in 1986 was that Bob, feeling some financial pressures, went to visit his father, Merlin Spangler, back in Ames, Iowa. The elder Spangler was now 92 years old but in fine health.

A few days after Bob arrived at his father's home, the elder

Spangler took a terrible fall. He was dead within two weeks. Bob inherited a tidy sum and was able to retire.

Sharon's Problems

But Sharon's mental and emotional problems continued to escalate, and it was wearing on their marriage.

In December 1987, Sharon made a frantic, incoherent call to the police, saying she was afraid of Bob. She ran from the house into a local supermarket and hid in a stock room. She struggled with police when they tried to take her out of the grocery store, convinced that Bob was out to "get her," and it's uncertain if she was justifiably terror-struck or if her medications were out of whack. Regardless, she and Bob divorced soon thereafter.

The divorce settlement was hard on Bob. It included spousal support payments to her of $500 per month until 1990, and then $400 per month until July 1997. She took another $150,000 in compensation from stocks and bonds, and they each had visitation rights with the three dogs, although Sharon took Shadow and left Sunshine and Mollie with Bob.

There was one strange clause to the divorce decree, and that was that Bob was to receive $20,000 back from her estate should Sharon predecease him.

It was an expensive divorce for him—in fact he had to go back to work—but he didn't seem to be able to quite sever ties with Sharon. Not then, and not for a long time.

Sharon moved on and found Michael, another equally distressed soul to increasingly complicate her life.

Bob, single again at age 55, frantically sought a new mate. He started by placing a personals ad.

The Third Wife

Donna Sundling, an aerobics instructor with five grown children from nearby Evergreen, Colorado, answered his ad. Donna fell head over heels in love with Bob, and was willing to do just about anything for him.

The first thing she did was marry him on August 18, 1990, after a whirlwind courtship. Then he convinced her to sell her expensive, upscale home and move with him to Durango, Colorado, apparently, on a whim.

There he got a job as the morning drive time on-air personality for KRSJ, a country music station where he grew to enormous popularity. According to *The Durango Herald*, He also worked part time as a referee for Durango Parks and Recreation, officiating at youth and adult basketball and soccer games.

Bob was crazy for hiking the Grand Canyon, and their home was filled with large framed photos of the canyon, left over from his days with Sharon.

Donna was fit, and willing to do about anything for him, but besides suffering from vertigo, she was afraid of heights. A fitness instructor is not the same as a strong hiker, and at 56 years old, she struggled to keep up with her super-fit (and proud of it) husband on some canyon hikes that scared her. She used ski poles to help keep her balance on the trails. She did it, but she didn't like it. She did it for him.

Eventually, she didn't go with him as often as he would have liked, and he sought out other hikers to join him on his treks.

It wasn't long before Bob knew this marriage was in trouble, too. Donna just wasn't what he expected. She wasn't what he wanted any more.

But divorce… divorce was expensive, as he had already discovered with Sharon.

She knew their marriage was in trouble, too, and in an effort to save it, she agreed to one more Grand Canyon hike with him.

A Tragic Accident

On Easter Sunday, April 11, 1993 a disheveled but strangely calm Bob Spangler showed up at the Back Country ranger station, saying that his wife had taken a tragic fall. She was dead 160 feet below the Redwall at Horseshoe Mesa, where they had stopped for a photo. He set up his camera to take a photograph of them both, and when he turned back around, she had vanished. He had heard nothing.

When he saw her broken body lying motionless beneath him, he scrambled down, found her dead, washed the blood from her face with his handkerchief, covered her with a tarp, grabbed her pack and headed back up to report the tragedy.

The rangers snickered about "Divorce by Grand Canyon," but there was no evidence of foul play, despite the fact that the place she fell was probably the only place on their hiking route that would have resulted in a fatal fall. And the fact that he never heard her cry out when she went over was an odd detail they couldn't quite forget.

When he got home, the distraught Spangler called John Mackley, his boss at the radio station, and told him that Donna had fallen in the Grand Canyon and died, and that Spangler wouldn't be in to work.

He had her cremated right away.

Donna left behind five grieving children and five grandchildren.

Mackley and his wife, along with all the Spanglers' friends and coworkers attended the memorial service Bob designed, at which he eulogized her at length. One friend called the service "tearless and weird."

Spangler even went back to the Grand Canyon to scatter wildflower seeds at "Donna's Point," the place at which she died. The grieving husband also went on local talk shows, discussing the dangers of hiking in the canyon. He was quoted in *USA Today* and on *NPR*.

Afterwards, he confided in John Mackley that his teenage son David had gone crazy back in 1978 and killed Bob's wife and daughter, then turned the gun on himself.

When Mackley related this information to his wife, Pam remembers saying, "How much can one poor man endure?"

It wasn't the first time Spangler had changed the facts of

that story, and it wouldn't be the last. He told others that his whole family had died in a terrible car accident in which he was the driver and sole survivor.

The Lonely Widower, Part II

While Bob was busy with his failing marriage to Donna, second wife Sharon's life was falling apart. Michael, her boyfriend, was even in worse shape than she was, and when Bob reopened communications and told her about Donna's death, Sharon thought she might be able to lean on Bob, as always. Besides, she needed the comfort only her dogs could provide, so in July 1994, she came to visit him in Durango and ended up staying in Bob's guest room.

But it didn't help. Shadow, her dog and best friend, died, and Sharon was inconsolable. She spent day after day crying and mourning the loss.

Bob, meantime, was the happiest disc jockey Durango had ever seen. Always ebullient, upbeat to a fault, he coached soccer and hiked local trails, always with a smile on his face. He reveled in his minor celebrity.

John Mackley, his boss at the small radio station, never even knew Bob had a wife between Nancy and Donna, much less that she was back living with him. Spangler never once mentioned her to any of his coworkers.

And then on October 2, 1994, just five months after moving back in with Bob, the 52-year-old Sharon's grief became too much for her to bear. She took an overdose of prescription medication and left a note on her bedroom door, "I've done it this time."

From there, the details get sketchy. As usual, Bob would change his story. One version he told had him come home, see the note, try to rouse an unresponsive Sharon, and he carried her immediately to the emergency room. In another version, he came home, saw the note, but didn't pay any attention to it until much later, when he went into her room, found her groggy, and helped her into the car and took her to the emergency room.

What is certain, is that she died a few hours after being treated in the hospital. Again, details are foggy. One account says that the doctors who treated her thought she'd be fine, but she was left alone in a room for a while with Spangler just before she died.

Regardless, she did die, there was no investigation into her death, and Spangler no longer had to pay the spousal support. He also got the $20,000 back from her estate (had to file a lawsuit to get it), as had been stipulated in their divorce agreement, and he had her cremated right away.

His co-workers at the small radio station never knew. They never knew he had another wife, never knew she was living with him after Donna's death, never knew he had taken her to the emergency room, never knew she had died.

Even he must have thought that would sound like one too many dead wives.

Bill Burnett, one of Donna's friends, certainly thought so, and phoned a friend in law enforcement to look into it.

Desperately Seeking

In 1998, Spangler suddenly quit his job at the radio station, sold everything (he had inherited Donna's half of their Durango home) and moved to Pennsylvania to pursue a woman he had met over the internet.

That particular relationship didn't pan out, but he was on the move, on the hunt, and he relentlessly pursued women, desperate to be married again. His favorite date was a hike in the Grand Canyon, but by now, he was being watched by the police. They were afraid there would be another Grand Canyon "accident."

Bob eventually moved to Grand Junction, Colorado, to pursue a woman whose interest in him began to wane. He continued to encourage her while dating others. He didn't have time to waste. By the time he met Judy Hilty at a breakfast for singles, he was working as Vice President of Applecrest

Irrigation company and dabbling in community theater.

He and Judy were instantly attracted to each other, and all other women fell into the background.

Then he had a little trouble with his eyesight. Then he couldn't remember his lines in play rehearsals, and had some trouble concentrating. He went to the doctor on August 12, 2000 and got the bad news. Inoperable lung cancer which had spread to his brain. Spangler was 67.

On September first, he and Judy married.

The cops moved closer. They were afraid Judy was about to have an accident.

Brilliant police work

The first time the police went to visit Bob was right after Sharon's death, in August, 1995.

Alerted by one dead wife too many, investigations were reopened into the death of Nancy and her children by the Arapahoe County police. Investigator Paul Goodman began working in conjunction with Investigator Bev Perry with the FBI on the death of Donna on federal lands in the Grand Canyon.

Bob was not surprised to see the police, and invited the investigators in, spoke calmly with them about the tragedies that had befallen him.

He continued to change the details of his stories, and when asked about that, he said, "I compartmentalize things and don't live in the past."

Investigators left him, but behind-the-scenes work had just begun.

It required an amazing coordination of efforts since he was being investigated for not only a Colorado state murder case, but also a Federal murder. And then there were the suspicious deaths of both his father and his second wife, Sharon.

Over the years, the Spangler file began to build with questionnaires sent to many Durango residents and the re-examination of old forensic evidence with up-to-date technology. Camille Bibles, Assistant United States Attorney, was now involved, and the wheels of justice began to grind a little more rapidly.

But once his terminal diagnosis was confirmed, they had no choice but to make their move.

The Confession

The way to handle Spangler, the investigators realized, was to play to his enormous ego. When they finally knocked on the door of his Grand Junction home and invited him to the police station for questioning, they had already set the stage.

Spangler had to walk past boxes and boxes marked "Spangler Task Force." This pleased him.

The police began by telling him that they'd never investigated a killer quite like him before.

His response? "It requires a singular focus in committing the actual crime, quite cold-bloodedly," Spangler said.

Facing death by cancer, he was eager to unburden himself, and readily confessed to the killing of Nancy and the children. Strangely enough, he wanted to confess these crimes to a profiler, who could perhaps answer a few questions about himself. He was adopted, he said. He didn't know how he could have behaved the way he had.

Investigators said that profilers only spoke to serial killers—those who had killed more than three people. Apparently, one had to be a real killer for an interview with a profiler. Just killing three wasn't good enough.

Spangler was fascinated with the idea of talking with a profiler. He thought about that for a moment, then asked to speak privately with his wife. They agreed, and let Bob and Judy have some time alone together.

When he returned, he said, "You've got your serial."

What Really Happened: Nancy and the Kids

By 1974, Bob Spangler was bored out of his mind. His kids were out of control, his wife had a life of her own, but he was just a worker bee, droning through life.

Then he met Sharon at work. She was vivacious and sparkly, and he was more than smitten with her, he was obsessed. He moved out of the house, and for nine months he rarely even saw the children. He was busy with his new life, his new love.

But divorce was going to be horribly expensive after all those years of marriage. There had to be another way.

Slowly, a cure for his problems began to formulate in his mind.

He moved back in with Nancy and the kids to try to reconcile, or so he told everyone. The kids had lost respect for him and weren't shy about offering up that opinion.

He carefully set the stage for his little play, typing a suicide note on the typewriter in the basement. He told Nancy it was a Christmas letter and set it in front of her. Without reading it, she signed her initial. Then he staged a big fight with her on the evening of December 29, and made sure that there were witnesses to it.

Then on December 30, he placed a footstool in front of the open closet door where he kept his .38 revolver and lured Nancy to the basement. He had her sit in front of the typewriter, told her he had a surprise for her, and to close her eyes. Excitedly, she did as she was told, and he shot her in the forehead.

Then he sneaked upstairs and shot Susan once in the back.

David was more difficult, because Bob had to shoot him in the chest, and David didn't die right away. He wrestled with his dad, but Bob couldn't shoot him again, because he knew Nancy wouldn't have done that.

So he smothered his son with the boy's own pillow.

Then Bob left the house, drove around for a while and eventually went to see the animated "Lord of the Rings."

"It seemed like a good idea at the time," he said of the massacre.

What Really Happened: Donna

It wasn't long after Bob married fitness instructor Donna

that he realized she was not the woman for him. He met her via a personals ad, and while she had seemed perfect, time proved that they had nothing in common. There was only her undying devotion to him.

Bob was eager to show to everyone, particularly the women in his life, his athletic prowess, but Donna didn't enjoy hiking in the Grand Canyon, and it had become his life.

He knew, from his expensive experience divorcing Sharon, that Donna would likely take him to the cleaners, especially since he had encouraged her to sell her very nice Evergreen home and put all that money into the Durango house.

There was a solution to his unhappiness, he knew, that would be easier than divorce.

He finally succeeded in talking her into taking another Grand Canyon trip with him and masterminded his plan on the way. They would hike a trail that went past the Redwall on Horseshoe Mesa, a ledge that was perfect for the crime—in that the drop off was so severe—that she was certain to die when she hit bottom.

Even Sharon, the Grand Canyon expert, was afraid of that area.

Bob queried hikers they met on the trail to make certain they wouldn't be camping in the same vicinity, and in fact he and Donna camped on an illegal site, just to make certain of it.

The next morning, Easter Sunday, he decided it was "now or never," and shoved her over the edge while she was looking him right in the face.

Then he climbed down to her, perhaps to make certain she was dead, and to complete the task if she was not. He cleaned the blood off her face, covered her with a tarp and went to the authorities.

He said their marriage had been a mistake.

The Plea

Except for just those two bad days, Spangler told investigators, he'd been a model citizen.

He denied all responsibility in the death of Sharon.

But on November 5, 2000, he pled not guilty, intimating that his brain cancer had led him to make faulty confessions.

The Arapahoe County district attorney's office consulted with Nancy's family and determined it would be a waste of money to bring him to Colorado for trial in the murder of his Littleton, Colorado family.

"It just didn't seem like a prudent expenditure," prosecution spokesman Michael Knight said, since Spangler had an apparent month or so left to live.

The families agreed. David Fitch, Nancy Spangler's half-brother said, "If the man truly has terminal cancer, it's very unlikely he'd survive until the end of the trial."

Spangler eventually signed a plea agreement, to serve life in prison for Donna Sundling's first-degree murder.

His request to have his ashes spread in the Grand Canyon was denied.

Judy Hilty Spangler stood by her man until the very end. She said her husband had told her that his prior marriages had ended tragically, but she never suspected he was involved in their deaths. "I had no idea he was capable of this sort of thing," she said. "He always seemed a very gentle person."

Bob Spangler died in the Federal Corrections Medical Center in Springfield, Missouri, at 3:15am on August 5, 2001, ten months after being taken into custody, and 23 years after killing Nancy and the kids.

Bibliography

Married to Murder by Robert Scott, (2004, Pinnacle Books)

The FBI Law Enforcement Bulletin — "Resurrecting cold case serial homicide investigations (Robert Spangler Case)" by Camille Bibles

Denver Rocky Mountain News — "Killer of Three Won't be Tried" 1/18/2001

Denver Rocky Mountain News — "Slaying Suspect Taken to

Arizona" 10/11/2000

The Mirror — "Dying Man: I'm a Killer" 10/21/2000

Denver Rocky Mountain News — "Man Who Admits Killing Four" 10/22/2000

Denver Rocky Mountain News — "Confession Shocks 4th Spouse" 10/7/2000

Denver Rocky Mountain News — "Spangler Confession" 10/22/2000

Denver Rocky Mountain News — "Man 68, Guilty of Killing Wife" 12/28/2000

Denver Rocky Mountain News — "Terminally Ill Man Admits" 10/5/2000

Denver Rocky Mountain News — "Suspect's Eulogy 'Weird'" 10/6/2000

Denver Rocky Mountain News — "Technician Let Killer Sleep Over" 10/18/2000

Denver Rocky Mountain News — "Suspect in Wife's 1993 Death" 11/8/2000

Durango Herald — "Dying Man Says" 10/6/2000

Durango Herald — "Spangler to Stay in Jail" 10/7/2000

Durango Herald — "Father Questioned Spangler's Suicide" 10/12/2000

Durango Herald — "Spangler Pleads Innocent" 11/8/2000

Durango Herald — "Spangler Pleads Guilty" 12/28/2000

Durango Herald — "Spangler Sentenced" 3/13/2001

Denver Post — "For Suspected Killer" 10/8/2000

Gabriel Morris:

Mormon, Missionary, Murderer

The hatred of relatives is the most violent.
— *Tacitus (c. 55 - c. 117)*

One February Night

At daybreak, on February 8, 2010, 33-year-old Gabriel Morris, his wife Jessica, and their four-year-old daughter drove the red GMC pickup truck that they had borrowed from Jessica's father up the long. wooded driveway toward the house where Gabe's mother lived with her boyfriend. The clutch was almost gone, and they were running on fumes.

Gabe parked and handed his wife one of their walkie-talkies. He took the other, and a pair of binoculars, then stealthily walked around the back of the property to the tree line, where he waited to see activity in the house, indicating that his mother and her boyfriend were up and about on this Monday morning.

Jessica, misunderstanding a radio transmission from her husband, started the truck and drove up toward the house, where Gabe met her and angrily directed her to drive instead down a spur road that wound around and ended up behind the garage, a parking area that was not visible from the house. Gabe went back to his surveillance while Jessica spent over six hours in the cab of the truck trying to entertain their four-year-old. Gabe didn't want to see his mom, Robin Anstey, or her boyfriend, Bob Kennelly, at least not on their terms. When

Kennelly Home—Bandon, OR
Police evidence photo

that meeting took place, Gabe wanted to be in control. He needed to have the upper hand for the little chat he told his wife that he intended to have with them.

Gabe and his family had been living in Kennelly's nicely appointed two-story home that faced the river since September, but tensions had ratcheted up to the point where Gabe and Jessica took off on a spontaneous road trip for about a week to escape what they perceived as a dangerous situation, to clear their heads, to think through their options, to decide what their next step ought to be.

But on February 8, they were back, weary from traveling and needing both food and sleep.

Gabe didn't like the way his mother and her boyfriend treated him and his family, and he told Jessica that their next step was to have a good airing of the issues. Have a chat. Get everything out in the open.

But when that meeting took place, he'd be in complete control of it.

So he waited in the woods and his wife waited in the truck for his mother and her boyfriend to leave the house.

Eventually, Robin and Bob left, and Gabe went inside. He got Bob Kennelly's .40 magnum Heckler and Koch semi-automatic handgun from the safe inside the walk-in closet of the bedroom he had been sharing with his wife, indicating that he anticipated something other than a friendly chat or family meeting with his mom and her boyfriend. After a few more hours, he told Jessica that he'd be more comfortable if she was in the house too, so she and their little girl went inside, got something to eat, then Jessica and Kalea put on their pajamas and went upstairs to bed.

Sometime around 8:30 that evening, after having dinner with friends, Bob and Robin returned home and walked through the French doors into the house. Robin set her purse and packages down on the couch, and from the upstairs balcony, Gabe, the devoted husband, the devout Mormon, the ex-police officer and former missionary opened fire.

Bob Kennelly and Robin Anstey
Victims Photos

There was no discussion about money. There was no little chat about how they'd been treated. There were no accusations or defenses; there was only an ambush and a rain of gunfire.

He continued to shoot as he walked along the balcony and down the stairs. Bob fell just inside the door. Gabe's mother made it out the door, screaming, before he put a bullet in her butt that shattered her hip. He ended Bob's pain, as he later described it, then when he got to his mother, he was out of ammunition, so he dropped the empty clip as he was trained to do as a police officer, reloaded, and put a bullet in her head that sprayed her molars out onto the deck.

When Gabe was finished, his 62-year-old mother and her 48-year-old boyfriend lay dead. Gabe turned his mother over, just to make sure.

Gabe ran back upstairs into the bedroom and merely said, "Let's go." His hustled his terrified wife and screaming child down the stairs. He stopped to go through the dead man's pants pockets for the keys to Kennelly's car and his wallet, then all of them shoeless, two of them in their pajamas, they stepped over the bodies and walked out into the February night. They got into Bob Kennelly's white Dodge truck and spit gravel as Gabe sped recklessly down the steep driveway and into town.

Gabe knew exactly where to go. He knew precisely who to contact and what to ask for once he got there. He knew exactly how to ask for it, and he knew that he'd get it, too. It appears as if those plans had been very carefully laid, well in advance.

Strangely, none of this information was ever in dispute, not even by Morris himself. What was in question was his state of mind for the two weeks leading up to the murders and, indeed, events in his life that molded him into the person who could behave in such a manner.

Is Gabe Morris a cold-hearted killer, or a good man who fell victim to a progressive, debilitating mental illness?

The Pressure Cooker

Gabriel Christian Morris began life on September 22, 1976

in San Diego, California. His mother, Robin, already had a six-year-old son, Jesse, when Robin hooked up with and married Gabe's father, Danny Morris. Whereas Jesse was an easy baby, a delightful child who grew to be a compassionate man without a jealous, angry or vindictive bone in his body, Gabe was a difficult child, a terror, a maniac, even at two years old. He broke toys just to break them. As he grew older, he was a loving boy, but needed a disproportionate amount of attention from his mother. He was also quick to take roughhousing to the level of pain. "Mom called Gabe 'the devil child,'" Jesse McCoy said.

Both Gabe and his father have been described as "scary smart." According to family members, Danny Morris was kind of strange, intense, nervous and twitchy. He wasn't offensive or frightening, but he was tough on his stepson Jesse, and overly devoted to Gabe. He loved playing Dungeons and Dragons and introduced Gabe to gaming. Gabe called him "insanely intelligent," but manipulative, persuasive, controlling, cruel, and abusive. He took offense at every slight. Danny worked a variety of jobs, including in a bakery, at a sheet metal plant, and for a while he dealt drugs. When Danny and Robin began to have marital problems, Danny moved out, then filed for custody, lying about Robin being a drug dealing addict and an unfit mother. He was granted custody and Gabe was removed from her home and sent to live with Danny, who Gabe said sexually abused him. Jesse, out of concern for Gabe's safety, went to live with his brother as well.

Danny frequently told Gabe that his mother had just gone off and left him, continually reinforcing those deep, dark feelings of abandonment. Gabe never knew of her fight to regain custody. In return, Gabe wrote long Mother's Day cards to Robin and professed his love for her with a fierce intensity that his brother, Jesse, thought made his own devotion to his mother pale in comparison. Were these the desperate cries for acceptance from a child who felt abandoned? That ferocious adoration continued throughout his life. Everyone says Gabe adored his mother, but it went much further than that. He wanted her to adore him. He wanted her to love him enough to compensate him for the years he spent at his father's abusive hands.

She never could.

Gabe says his father abused him. Since Danny is now deceased, that is difficult information to corroborate, although some family members are convinced that this is true. At one point, Danny cried because Gabriel wanted to spend the night with a neighborhood friend instead of being at home with him. Even Gabe's brother, Jesse, said that Danny obsessed over Gabe, loving him way too much. During those summers, Gabe went to stay with his grandmother in Silverton, Oregon, and she said that Danny sent Gabe long love letters more suitable for a spouse than for a child. Pretty little blond Gabe, who spoke with an adorable lisp was not allowed to wear underwear and was required to sleep nude in his father's bed at night.

Later, Gabe would rage about his mother abandoning him and leaving him in the hands of an abuser, calling her evil. Yet, to all outward appearances, Gabe adored his mother and constantly worried for her safety.

Robin had her issues. She was born to Lynn and Martin Walsh in 1947 in Pontiac, Michigan. She had an older half-sister, Laurie, and a younger brother Scott, born in 1958 after the family moved to California. Robin's relationship with her father was always strained. He was a highly regimented pilot in World War II who demanded certain standards from his family members, and she was a young, carefree hippie girl in the 60s. When a teenager, she ran off and married John McCoy, who was in the Navy. After John was discharged, the couple was footloose and fun loving. Robin's parents bought their young son Jesse his first pair of shoes and gave him his first haircut, two things Robin didn't think were really very necessary at the time but served to distance even her further from her disapproving father. Robin was talented and artistic, earthy and sexy, but perhaps because of her difficult relationship with her harsh, alcoholic father who always thought she should have done more with her life, she had serious problems with self esteem.

When Robin and John McCoy's marriage began to disintegrate, Robin immediately found another man, and then almost as quickly, found and married Danny Morris. When that fell apart, she moved to Coquille, Oregon and lived with John Lindegren, "Big John," a smart, witty carpenter and American history buff who helped raise Gabe until he finished high school. Then she met and married James Anstey. Together, they owned a gift and antiques shop in Bandon, Oregon, a small coastal community that relies heavily on seasonal tourism. Robin had the ability to turn trash into treasure and the artistically displayed items they sold made "Hidden Treasures" a financial success.

Gabe referred to James Anstey as "the father he never had." After Robin and James' 10-year marriage ended, Robin immediately moved in with Bob Kennelly. It was there that she met her death.

She always needed to have a man in her life and went from one man's home and bed to the next in rapid succession. Perhaps her lack of discrimination gave Gabe reason to fear for her safety. Perhaps Gabe's perception that her choice of the man of the hour over his welfare gave him reason to rage against her.

Robin regained custody of Gabe from Danny in time for Gabe to begin high school in Bandon, Oregon, where she lived with Lindegren. In school, Gabe met and began dating Esther Eschler, a Mormon girl with eight siblings whose parents both worked in the school system. Here, Gabe had found a stable, loving family structure he could relax into. He and Esther dated for several years while he studied and ultimately converted to the Mormon faith. Fred Eschler, Esther's father, baptized him into the Church of Jesus Christ of Latter-Day Saints and welcomed Gabe into the family, gave him the run of the house, took him on family vacations with them, and generally treated him as one of his own. Before Esther, Gabe was known to smoke a little dope, but once he embraced the Mormon faith, he gave that up.

After high school graduation in 1996, Gabe moved in with his grandmother in Silverton, Oregon and went through the automotive program at Mt. Hood Community College, where he worked part time at the BMW dealership as a part of the curriculum. He completed the two-year program in 1998, then applied for and was accepted for a mission to spread the gospel of Jesus and the tenets of the Mormon Church in Australia. He was, according to Dr. Barry, the Mission President, an "exceptional young man among exceptional young men." This is a theme that runs through all the memories of everyone who knew Gabe as a youth. Kind-hearted. Sincere, Helpful. Honest. Incredibly smart. A good boy, grown to become a good kid, and finally, a good young man with excellent prospects for his future. Gabe seemed to take his faith seriously, a little too seriously for some in his family, but hey, there were worse things he could be into. If asked he'd say, "All I want to do is help people." These are golden words to those in his Mormon community, wherein helping people is a way of life.

But there were dark storm clouds brewing behind young Gabe Morris's eyes. Over the years, the compliments turned sour. He became known as a real bullshitter, a gifted salesman, who could talk for hours and never really say anything. And then eventually, the descriptive terms turned to words like con artist, video game junkie, pot head, religious fanatic, manipulative, braggart, and volatile.

After returning from his two-year mission in Australia in 2001, he lived with his mother and James Anstey and worked as a waiter and bartender in a local restaurant. He eventually applied to Brigham Young University in Provo, Utah, and was accepted into the Air Force ROTC program. At first, he roomed with Carl Eschler, brother of Esther.

Then he met Jessica Pope.

Never a womanizer, good looking Gabe Morris was attracted to the company of more intellectual women, so it was somewhat of a surprise when he hooked up with sweet, trusting Jessica Pope. Jessica was devoutly Mormon, from a nice family in Blackfoot, Idaho, a dedicated English major, and oh by the way, she had $100,000 in cash in the bank as a settlement from an accident.

Quickly, Gabe and Jessica married in the Mormon Temple and used her money to buy a house.

Both in school at BYU, Gabe and Jessica invited Gabe's older brother, Jesse, and his wife to live with them.

Gabe's attendance at school eventually began to wane. While Jessica completed her studies, Gabe exited the Air Force ROTC program from which he had taken scholarship money. In ROTC, the four-year college degree is funded by scholarships and repaid through service as an officer in the Air Force upon graduation. Since Gabe dropped out of the program without finishing, that scholarship money now needed to be repaid. Instead of studying, Gabe went back to his adolescent habit of playing video games and talking one-upmanship stories with his brother, who had been in and out of the Army for twelve years. Brother Jesse had experience with top secret "special ops" missions, and he and Gabe loved to talk about it. Gabe drank a little beer as they chatted, and he told Jesse that it would be better if his wife didn't know about that part, as drinking beer wasn't in line with the Mormon faith.

Gabe spent a year in ROTC, and it is only after three years that cadets get their assignments. Gabe wanted pilot school and told everyone that he had been accepted into pilot training. This wasn't true, and as his lies began to catch up with him, he quit the program, telling Jessica's family that he didn't want to subject his wife to the stresses and rigors of being a military wife. He told his colonel that he had to leave the program to protect his mother in a way that law enforcement could not protect her. Jessica graduated, and in 2005 they sold the house at a loss, the rest of her cash having been frittered away.

Not only broke, but now in debt, the couple moved back to Blackfoot, Idaho, to be near Jessica's parents. Gabe worked for a while at the Idaho State Mental Hospital as a psychiatric technician trainee. He enjoyed this job, working directly with psychiatric patients. Later, Gabe attended and graduated from the Idaho Police Academy and joined the Bingham County Sheriff's Department as a patrol deputy, about the same time he and Jessica welcomed the birth of their daughter, Kalea. From all outward appearances, life was smooth again for Gabe and his little family.

According to newspaper records, Gabe fit in well with the police department, but when someone else got the promotion to detective that he thought should be his, he quit the force in 2007, telling his supervisor that he got a job in Alaska as a bush pilot. He complained to his brother that he felt his life had been put into jeopardy during a raid, and that his fellow officers unfairly trapped suspects. He told a variety of stories to a variety of people about why he left the force, all continuing what had started to become a pattern of not sticking with much of anything and blaming everyone else for his failures. As soon as things didn't go quite his way, he quit. This time, as with the Air Force, he was required to reimburse the department for his training at the academy as he didn't fulfill his contract with the required years of service.

But when he left the force, he left with good solid training in firearms and the ways of police work. Might it also be safe to say that a "scary-smart" guy like Morris also left his employment at the state mental hospital with a good idea of what mental illness looks like?

He went to work at Gold's Gym in Blackfoot, where, true to his fast-talking, charismatic nature, he charmed all the clients, and a woman named Allie Smith in particular. One of the Gold's Gym clients recognized a good salesman in Gabe and offered him a job with American Family Insurance. Gabe took the job and hired Allie Smith to work for him, eventually telling her that he and Jessica were divorcing, igniting a romantic relationship that took the two of them on trips to Las Vegas, spending money neither of them had. Gabe lied to her, saying that he sold antiques for his stepfather, James Anstey. Gabe even went so far as to move to Pocatello and file divorce

Kalea, Gabe, and Jessica Morris
Family Photo

papers, which were never completed. Somehow, Gabe acquired access to Allie's credit cards and quickly ran up $30,000 worth of charges instead of tending to the insurance business, all the time telling his supervisors that things were going well.

But things weren't going very well with Gabe and Allie Smith.

In 2009, he returned to his wife, who took him back after he lied to her that he and Smith had not been romantically involved. Jessica believed him. She wanted to believe him. She wanted her daughter to have a father. She wanted a family.

Needless to say, Jessica's parents were none too thrilled with their son-in-law, particularly after Allie Smith began calling them, looking for her money. "He's a real scumbag," Rita Pope said in a newspaper interview. "He makes Tiger Woods look like a saint." The Air Force was looking for its scholarship money. The police department was looking to be repaid for his training. The insurance company was discovering that he was not making the sales he claimed to be making, and the squeeze was on to pay for the Mercedes he bought for Allie and the BMW he bought for himself to impress his insurance agency clients. In a few short years, Gabe had blown through Jessica's settlement, racked up about $100,000 in debt and had no job.

When her parents tried to talk to Jessica about Gabe, she wouldn't hear of it, according to a *Register-Guard* interview. "She thought she could make a responsible, hard-working fella out of him. Those two characteristics never seemed to appear," Bill Pope said. "She had all the faith in the world in God and his ability to transform people. It never happened. The subject of Gabe was kind of off limits for family discussion."

The pressure mounted and Gabe began to drink.

A Fresh Start

Back in Bandon, Oregon, Gabe's mother, Robin Anstey, had a house on Bowman Way that was falling into disrepair. She had just divorced James Anstey, they had closed the Hidden

Treasures shop and were liquidating all the antiques that had been put into storage. Robin was living with Bob Kennelly in his nice home in the woods, and it was always their plan to fix up the Bowman Way house and sell it, but the real estate market wasn't good. Gabe thought he might be able to help her with that. They could fix up the living space over the garage and live there and rent out the main house. Jessica thought they might turn it into a bed and breakfast. Maybe he and Jessica and Kalea could move there and he could quit drinking, work on the house and help James Anstey with his antiques business. Jessica could get a job and they could file bankruptcy and start over, fresh.

Reluctantly, Jessica's father agreed that a fresh start was in order. He loaned the kids his red GMC pickup truck and $5,000 in cash and wished them well. They packed up their daughter and in September of 2009, the family drove to Bandon.

Bandon by the Sea, as it calls itself in tourism publications, is a picturesque little coastal town on Highway 101. It sits on the banks of the Coquille River, renowned for its seasonal salmon runs. Bandon, the little town of Coquille, and the larger town of Coos Bay are all located in Coos County, a heavily wooded area of Oregon hit hard by the economic downturn in the logging industry. There's a nice casino in Coos Bay and a world-class golf course in Bandon, all of which helps bring tourist dollars to the area that is so depressed. Its saving grace is the fact that it is located on arguably the most beautiful coastline in the country, and in the summer, visitors in RVs and campers file up and down Highway 101, taking in the sights and filling the hotels and campgrounds to participate in all the beach and ocean activities. But in the winter months, the coast is cold, windy, foggy and rainy.

The Morrises arrived at Robin and Bob's home in September, 2009, eight miles inland from Bandon on Bob's 28 acres that included a beautiful shingled 2,800-square-foot two-story home that faced the Coquille River, a detached six-car garage/shop with offices and living space above, a barn and several other outbuildings. Bob raised alpacas and goats on the acreage and spent most of his time maintaining the property that he bought in 2008 after his second wife died of cancer.

The house had vaulted ceilings and a turret, which they referred to as the "castle room." A large iguana resided in an enormous cage on one side of the well-appointed living room which was filled with antiques and Robin's artistic touches. French doors led out to a wrap-around deck, with a hot tub in a gazebo. Inside, the spacious kitchen had oak cabinets and granite countertops.

Bob and Robin occupied the master suite on the ground floor, and they had Gabe, Jessica and Kalea move into an upstairs bedroom across from the upstairs bathroom. The bedroom next to theirs was used as storage, and down the hallway, which opened as a balcony to the kitchen and living room below, was the castle room, where Gabe played video games, smoked pot and watched Kalea during the day while Jessica worked as a bookkeeper, taught seminary classes at the local LDS church, and volunteered at the Women's Safety and Resource Center in Coos Bay.

Upstairs in the castle room, Gabe started smoking a lot of pot. He and Bob bought a pound with the intent to sell it to make a few bucks, but Gabe smoked his half in a bong he kept in the castle room, where he went online every day and played Perfect World, an online fantasy game with dragons and queens and quests that began in a time before humans and ends in apocalypse. Gabe had always been a gamer, beginning in his high school years, continuing through his time in Provo, but now he was a stay-at-home dad, and he had all the time he wanted to delve into his fantasy worlds. Bob, not a pot smoker, put his half pound into one of the two safes he kept in the house and eventually traded it for an ivory statue that he intended to sell.

But since pot was expensive, Gabe talked Bob and Robin into getting Oregon medical marijuana cards so they could buy it as patients. Robin, not a pot smoker either, had whiplash

Balcony in Kennelly's Home
Police Evidence Photo

from an old automobile accident, Bob claimed some injury, and Gabe put down a shoulder injury he received while on the police force as their required pain management issues and the three of them drove to Medford, filed their paperwork and received their cards. They also got a permit to grow marijuana to sell to other card-holding patients or caregivers as well as to a new medical marijuana clinic that was soon to open in Coos Bay.

They bought building materials, built a secure room inside the garage and began a small-scale marijuana grow. Somewhere along the line, Bob Kennelly loaned Gabe $25,000 with which to launch their business, and that debt became a bone of contention between them.

Gabe even contacted James Anstey with a business proposal: He'd go to Nevada and steal things, then Anstey could sell them in Oregon. Anstey declined and tried to talk some sense into Gabe, telling him that he was on the path to destruction. But Gabe didn't listen.

Tensions in the house began to escalate over the few months the Morrises lived in the house. Gabe didn't like the fact that his mother was living "in sin" with Bob without being married. Bob didn't like fact that Gabe and his family were living there without paying anything toward the household expenses. Robin confided in Jessica that she didn't want to be living with Bob, but she needed a man in her life. "I can't just leave him and go back to my own house and be by myself. That scares me more than staying here," Robin said.

Then came the day that Jessica started to feel ill. She got dizzy in the kitchen and Gabe convinced her that Bob Kennelly was putting rat poison in their food. At first, she was skeptical, but there was rat poison in the utility room, and Gabe showed her a white residue on some of the dishes. While Gabe and his family fixed their meals at home, Robin and Bob ate out. And there was no question that she wasn't feeling right.

What they didn't know was that she was pregnant.

Gabe was the master of spinning tales out of thin air, and

he began to get very creative with his art. Soon, everything started to smell like rat poison to Jessica's sensitive nose.

Gabe told her that he was developing a new video game with someone in Brazil. His conversations with others began to be peppered with tales of his time in the Air Force, when he was in "black ops" (*Black Ops* is a popular video game). He talked of going to China for one last mission for the secret governmental agency he worked for. He said at one point that as soon as he told people that he worked for the government, or he worked for the military, they relaxed and were willing to help him. He said people "want a story. They want to think that I work for the government. They want to think I work for the military. They want to think something, so I go along." He used this bit of knowledge to great advantage. Gabe began what appears to be a very well conceived and systematic revisiting of all his old friends from the days before he got himself into so much trouble. He began to consciously lose a lot of weight.

Was his mental health deteriorating, or was he practicing an alibi and a new persona—one that was manic and seemed a little crazy—for a crime he knew he would inevitably commit?

He visited an old employer with his grandiose stories, saying that he could "take care of" any problem that might arise. The inference was clear, although the former employer had no idea why Gabe visited him. They hadn't seen each other in years.

He visited Pam Hansen, a woman he knew from church when he was a teen, and spun an outrageous story that in the pre-mortal days (part of the Mormon theology), she was his queen and they rode dragons together (dragons are a part of the Perfect World game). He said he was the forerunner of Christ's second coming. He had begun to perfect the rambling rants at this point, mixing fantasy and reality, queens and dragons with military secrets and working security for a prostitution ring. Looming over the whole morass was fear for his family: he had to protect his daughter from being molested by Bob Kennelly, he had to protect Jessica and Kalea from the rat poison Kennelly was feeding them, and he had to protect his mother, even though he thought she was in on Kennelly's rat poison scheme and therefore was a "lost cause."

Pam was concerned for Gabe but didn't think he was in any danger of harming himself or others. He was just really, really stressed out.

And yet when she heard about the murders, Pam Hansen knew exactly what to do. She called the police and told them about her latest chat with Gabe.

Jessica was involved in a woman's group at the Bandon LDS church, and it was around this time that Gabe came to the group and acted in an inappropriate manner. When confronted by the leaders of that particular church, he declared himself Christ and was invited to leave the building. This was not the exceptional young man that the Mormon community had known when he was a teen and a missionary.

Jessica's parents called Robin and told her about Gabe's money problems, but when she confronted him, he exploded in anger. Unbeknown to Jessica, Robin had asked Gabe to contribute to the household expenses, which Gabe thought was completely unfair, and he found their accounting suspicious. In a big blow up, Robin even showed Gabe the paperwork on his childhood custody case. She had not abandoned him. She tried to tell him how hard she fought for him, but he wasn't listening. He had held on to his abandonment issues for too long to give them up now. He told his brother that their mother was evil. He began to talk of Bob and Robin as bad people. And he began to convince Jessica that her parents were evil as well.

Toward the end of January, Gabe convinced Jessica that they needed to leave the house immediately, before any of them ingested more rat poison, so he sent Jessica to their room to grab a few possessions and get into the car. Jessica did as she was told.

They drove, with no apparent plan, to Medford, about three hours away. Jessica, loyal to a fault, was not happy about missing work at the bookkeeping office, especially as tax season approached, but there was no denying that she felt funny, and Gabe was very convincing.

Realizing they were ill-prepared for a road trip, they went back to the house the following day to pack up some belongings. Robin and Bob wanted an explanation as to why they were in such a hurry to leave, but Jessica was busy packing Kalea's things and making sure she had everything they were going to need, and Gabe was busy packing up a few things from the castle room. Jessica didn't want to talk to Robin. "I didn't want to say, 'Because I think your boyfriend's hurting us.'" Forty-five minutes later, they were out of the house and on their way to Silverton, to Gabe's grandmother's house, where they washed all of their belongings to get the stink of rat poison out of them.

Gabe said he wanted to talk with his uncle, Scott Walsh, to see if there was a way to get Robin safely out on her own, maybe back into her own fixed-up house, but when he called his uncle, all he did was rant about a business opportunity he thought Scott ought to invest in. There was never a word about helping Robin or getting the family back together. It was all a manic rant, a pathetic attempt to find some money.

They needed to find themselves a new place to live, too, because they couldn't live with Bob and Robin anymore. That good idea hadn't panned out as well as it had first seemed when they were in Idaho.

They went to church that Sunday and Gabe continued his systematic renewing acquaintances with his new persona. He went to see Mike Woods, the shop foreman at the BMW dealership where Gabe trained during his Mount Hood Community College days. In those days, Gabe was a calm, compassionate guy, and now he seemed delusional with multiple grandiose stories about his involvement with secret black ops units in the military.

He went to see David Bastian, with whom he served his mission in Australia. David said that Gabe used to be a sincere individual, but this time, seven years later, Gabe was very excitable, said he worked for a black ops agency cracking codes. He insisted on talking with David in private, began to talk about apocalyptic happenings in California and Utah (The online game Perfect World has an apocalyptic aspect). He said he wanted to move to Silverton and open a coffee shop so he could preach, and his wife wanted to open a bed and breakfast to help pay the bills. He talked nonstop about the $200,000 car he had bought to outrun the police, and then he began to say things about killing anyone who tried to molest his daughter. He said that people who had a lot of money and nice houses should share with people who don't have as much. That night, David was mildly troubled about this new Gabriel Morris, but he didn't think that Gabe was in any danger to himself or others. He just thought Gabe was going through some stressful times.

Gabe and his family continued their ill-conceived road trip of searching for a place to live, although they had no money to get started, and didn't have most of their belongings. They headed to Seattle, where Jessica unsuccessfully tried to borrow money from old friends, as she had served her LDS mission in the Seattle area. Then they headed back down south, pawning their wedding rings for gas money, talking about moving here and there, all the way to San Diego, where Gabe showed her the severely distressed neighborhood where he grew up.

New stories were continually added to his rant. Now Bob Kennelly was building a place where he could molest Kalea (the marijuana grow room they had built was secure and relatively soundproof). One of his wildest stories was that his father took him out into the ocean when he was four years old, dropped him in and left him to drown. He said he sank to the bottom, heard the voice of God and realized he could breathe underwater, so he just walked out of the ocean and back up the beach to the amazement of his parents.

And now he could heal.

They spent a week in a motel in San Diego, as surely all the old memories of a desperate childhood resurfaced. Abuse at the hands of his father and his older brother. Perceived abandonment by his mother. Perhaps a few things began to come into focus for him with regards to his mother's series of boyfriends and her current choice of Bob Kennelly over Gabe and his family.

Finally, on February 7, they moved everything out of the motel room and back into the red truck that Jessica's dad had loaned them and headed back to Oregon. Gabe said it was time to confront Bob about the rat poison and the way they were being treated. It just wasn't right.

Jessica went along with whatever Gabriel said. He was her husband. He was the father of her child. He was the head of their household. And if he wanted to smoke a little dope, well, that was okay because he had a medical marijuana card. It was medicinal.

They drove all night, pulling into Bandon at daybreak and creeping up the long driveway. Bob and Robin generally stayed up until 2 a.m. and slept until noon.

Gabe was adamant that he have the upper hand when he confronted them, so they parked behind the garage and for six hours, Jessica sat in the truck and tried to occupy the mind of her four-year-old while Gabe went into the woods to keep surveillance on the house until his mother and her boyfriend got up and left.

Eventually they did, and that was the last time they left the house alive.

On the Run

Gabriel took his terrified, disoriented family on a wild ride that February night after the shooting, sliding down the steep driveway, banging into the embankment until Jessica thought the truck would tumble off the side of the road and roll down into the river. When she asked him why he'd shot his mother and Bob, Gabe replied, "Because it had to be done." And that was explanation enough for her.

Gabe drove directly to the Eschler's neighborhood in

Coquille and parked a few houses down the street. Gabe knew that Fred Eschler had guns. He also knew that the Eschlers thought of him as a son, and that they were good-hearted people who would likely do anything for him in his hour of need.

He said to Jessica, "Follow along. Do what I say." And she did.

Fred and Laura Eschler were in the kitchen about 9 PM when the doorbell rang. Laura opened the door and moments later, Gabe was in the kitchen, talking with rational urgency to them. No mystical, magical, manic weirdness. He said that he'd been working undercover for a secret Air Force agency and that terrorists had killed his mother and Bob, and that he had shot one of them at the scene before he and his family escaped. A handgun fell out of his clothing as he talked, and he asked for .40 caliber ammunition for Kennelly's gun, and a ride to an Air Force base in California, where he could check in with his agency and find safety for his family.

Fred had no reason to disbelieve Gabe who was very aware and very much in control. Both Fred and his wife had to work in the morning, so he couldn't give them a ride, but they could take his car. He gave Gabe a Beretta 9 mm pistol and a shoulder holster, and together they loaded three magazines, while Laura cleaned some personal items out of their silver Ford Taurus and fixed them some food for their trip. They didn't have any shoes for Kalea, but Laura gave Jessica some thick socks for the girl, and warm clothes all around as well as whatever cash they had on hand, about eighty dollars. Jessica asked if they had a car seat, but Gabe said they wouldn't need one. He'd be down in the back seat with Kalea. Those who were after him would be looking for the white truck with three people. A silver Taurus with a lone woman driving would not be suspicious. When Fred asked more probing questions, Gabe countered with, "It's better for you not to know."

As they were leaving, Kalea looked up and said, "Something happened to Grandma."

"Let's not talk about Grandma," Gabe said and hustled his family out the door and into a car they knew nobody would be looking for. He and Kalea got down in the back seat and Jessica drove through the night toward San Diego.

Again, the conversation revolved around where they were going to go to make a fresh start.

Since they had left the Kennelly residence so suddenly, Jessica was without her purse, and Gabe had left without his wallet. They had no identification with them at all, so they drove straight through to the motel they'd stayed in the week before in San Diego, and Jessica was able to secure them a room for one night without identification as the desk clerk remembered her. Gabe disassembled Kennelly's gun and threw it out the window where it was recovered and turned in to the San Diego police department. The police had the custody of the gun before the bodies were discovered in Oregon. At one point, Jessica asked Gabe to drive past the Mormon Temple in San Diego so she could show Kalea, but Gabe refused. "It's just another building," he said. Instead, he pulled into a hospital parking lot and stole a California license plate from a similar Ford Taurus, but never got around to putting it on the Eschler's car.

Short on cash, Gabe robbed a business for traveling funds while Jessica and Kalea waited in the car, and then they headed east. In Yuma, they used two Wal-Mart gift cards, taken from Bob Kennelly's wallet, that totaled $170 for provisions, since they'd left with nothing. Kalea got some clothes and a car seat, and they bought toothpaste, soap, hair products and such. Gabe threw the rest of Bob's wallet out the window.

In Arizona, he robbed another business, and after that, they panhandled at truck stops, Jessica doing most of the begging. "She's very humble," Gabe said. Big-hearted truckers were willing to give her money for gas.

In Mesa, they spent the night with some of Jessica's LDS friends. Gabe lied to them about being in the Air Force, and said they were relocating from the east coast to the west coast, on their way to California. The next morning, they continued their odyssey around the country, restlessly looking for a place to land. He convinced Jessica that they could change identities and live normal lives. Their past was behind them now, and they had a good future ahead. She believed him. She didn't need to leave. She didn't need to call the police. He'd take care of his family, as the head of the household was supposed to do.

Occasionally they would stop at a public library to use a computer. Gabe was trying to connect with people he'd met online playing the fantasy game Perfect World. But while he connected here and there, nothing panned out as far as a place for them to stay.

Until they reached Michigan. Then Gabe sweet-talked fellow gamer Kelly Love and her husband Scott Snyder to meet him and Jessica in Washington, D.C.

Gabe had met Kelly in the Perfect World game and they talked and flirted via Skype. He told her he worked for the Air Force and he helped her with some ideas for graphics for her new website. So when he called and said he was traveling around, meeting some of his gamer friends, she wasn't surprised.

The Morrises arrived in Washington on February 14 with ten dollars to their names. They found Kelly and Scott in the bar of a pizza place. Kelly and Scott bought them dinner, and then at Gabe's persistent and persuasive urging, reluctantly agreed to let the family stay with them for a night. Kelly and Scott were living at the home of Scott's mother in Dumfries, Virginia.

Gabe told Jessica that he thought very highly of Kelly, that in the online gaming world, she had stuck up for him, and he hoped they would be able to give them a car and some money. Jessica didn't know that Gabe and Kelly had been engaging in an online flirtation, but that attraction blossomed when they got together in person. When they got to Kelly and Scott's place, Gabe discovered that Kelly was quite ill, and had been for some time with an intestinal ailment that made it difficult for her to eat.

Gabe offered to heal her.

This wasn't news to Jessica, as Gabe had healed her and Kalea many times before. "He's blessed in the ability to heal people. He's a priesthood holder in the church," she said.

Kelly wasn't sure about all of this, so she talked it over with her husband. Already she could sense that Gabe had a strong hold over his wife and that frightened her, as she felt herself becoming ensnared as well. She suspected that if Gabe really could heal her and he did, that he would have a powerful hold on her, too.

Gabe told Scott that he had been poisoned, that he deliberately ate the poison, an amount that would have killed an ordinary person, but because of his extraordinary powers granted by God, he was able to heal himself. Scott told Kelly said that receiving a blessing from Gabe couldn't hurt, and in fact it might help. Kelly was tired of being in pain.

So Gabe prayed over her and convinced her that he had the power to heal, and immediately, she felt better.

She began sleeping in their bed. Kelly, Gabe, Kalea and Jessica.

Soon, it was just Gabe and Kelly in the bed having sex during the day while Scott worked and Jessica and Kalea were elsewhere in the house. If Jessica happened to get near the room where Gabe and Kelly were having private time, he became furious, accusing his meek wife of spying on him.

So Jessica, in order to earn their keep, cooked for the family. And when more people came over and she hadn't cooked enough to feed everyone, she wouldn't eat.

Once, Kelly found Jessica sitting by an open window, and she took the opportunity to ask her if she ever doubted Gabe's actions or the things he said. Jessica said no, that she trusted him, and when her trust falters, it's a slip of her faith. Gabe told Jessica that her parents were evil and she had come to believe that. Kelly said later that she thought Jessica loved Gabe and wanted something that he wouldn't give her, which was his love.

After a week, Gabe sensed that it was time to move on. He wanted to go to Florida, where his brother Jesse lived with his family. He began to pressure Kelly and Scott to join them on the road. Kelly and Scott had money, they had a fresh car, and Gabe convinced Jessica that if they all traveled together, Jessica wouldn't have to beg for gas money any more. Kelly and Scott were going to help them.

But Scott said a flat no, and Kelly resisted. Gabe was insistent. He wanted Kelly to go with them. He began to do what had always worked for him in the past, amping up his fast-talking line. Saying he worked in a secret agency for the Air Force had motivated people to help him in the past, surely it would work again. But Kelly was skeptical. If they were so important to the Air Force, why were they so broke with no place to stay?

To try to convince her, Gabe confessed that he'd had to go so far as to kill his mother and her boyfriend, and Jessica confirmed it. He also said that his mother was a prostitute and never raised him. He told her that he grew up on the streets and never knew his father. He tried to help his mother by letting her move into his house in Bandon and she tried to poison him in return. She tried to kill him for a hundred thousand dollars, so he had his mother and her boyfriend kneel before him and he shot them both.

But Scott's mother worked for the police department. And when Gabe told Kelly that he had killed his mother, it didn't take long for this information to get to Scott's mom. She looked him up on the internet and found him on the America's Most Wanted television show website.

Unbeknownst to Gabe, Kelly looked through the bag he had stashed in the closet and found Fred Eschler's 9mm Berretta. Clearly, she telegraphed her fear, and after that, Gabe was with her at all times. Kelly never had the opportunity to be alone with her husband or her brother or anyone, because Gabe was always within earshot.

Gabe and Jessica had been with them for about a week.

Gabe could feel the net closing in on him and he began to talk hard and fast to Kelly, who had no idea what to do. She had no idea what he was capable of. A week ago, she was helping out a friend and his family and now she felt like a hostage. As Gabe got more and more agitated, life for Kelly turned dark and very, very frightening.

The Manhunt

Fred Escher called the police after Gabe and his family left his home, but as no homicides were outstanding, he was referred to the FBI. Terrorism was under the jurisdiction of the Federal Government, not Coos County.

February 10, two days after the murders, the Coquille police received a complaint that a white Dodge truck was illegally parked. A patrol officer was dispatched to look into the matter and when he traced the license plate, he drove to Robert Kennelly's house, where he could see the open French doors and a woman lying motionless on the deck. Upon closer examination, he could also see the body of Bob Kennelly.

He called for reinforcements.

Detective Daniel Looney responded with the Coos County Major Crime Team and with the help of the Oregon State Police Crime Laboratory, the house was carefully searched for evidence. The Heckler and Koch handgun case along with its purchase receipt was found in the safe in the Morris's bedroom. Through the computer network, its serial number matched a gun found in a grass strip alongside a street in San Diego. A nationwide manhunt was initiated to locate the main suspect, Gabriel Morris. He was considered armed and extremely dangerous. Jessica Morris was wanted as a material witness. The National Center for Missing and Exploited Children became involved in looking for Kalea Morris and sent flyers around the country. America's Most Wanted television show became interested and aired an episode on February 20.

Bob Kennelly was found face-up on the floor of the living room, with wounds to his lower leg and the back of his neck that indicated the trajectory of the bullets came from the balcony. The fatal wound cut through his liver and into his lung. This shot was fired as Kennelly lay on the ground. The shell casing fell onto his clothing.

Robin Anstey was found face-up on the deck, just outside the open French doors with wounds through her upper arm, her left leg and her buttocks. The fatal wound was to her head.

The Oregon State Major Crime Team used dowels with lasers on their ends to gauge the trajectory of all the bullets found in the furniture, walls and flooring. All in all, thirteen .40 caliber shell casings were found. There were bullet holes in the leaves of the umbrella plant that Gabe stood behind when he began firing, then he apparently leaned over the balcony, presumably for greater accuracy. Shell casings bounced off the wall and around the kitchen as he moved across the balcony and down the stairs. Bullet fragments were found in a candle bowl on the kitchen countertop and in a Christmas tree stand on the deck. Marijuana and smoking paraphernalia were found in the castle room, and 26 juvenile marijuana plants about 12" tall were found in the grow room in the garage where Kennelly kept a pristine '51 DeSoto.

Jessica's purse was found in the Pope's red truck, and Gabe's passport was in the castle room. Deep tire marks that spit gravel were grooved in a grassy area where they drove Bob Kennelly's truck recklessly down the steep driveway to escape the crime scene.

Parricide is the term used when a child kills a parent. Matricide is the murder of a mother; patricide is the killing of a father.

Some interesting statistics from *Why Kids Kill Parents* by Kathleen M. Heide, PhD:

- On average, about five parents are killed by their biological children in the US every week.
- Of the approximately 250 parents killed by their

children each year, about 100 of these victims are mothers.
- Most mothers who are slain by their offspring are killed by sons.
- Most matricides involve adult offenders.

Heide states: "In parricide cases, I have seen good parents overindulge their children with fatal results… [the child] has no frustration tolerance, meaning that he does not know how to deal with disappointment, and gets angry. Sometimes the anger is so intense that it erupts into deadly rage."

All evidence found at the Bandon house crime scene pointed to the eruption of smoldering rage. While Gabe seems to have carefully groomed those who would eventually testify on his behalf of his craziness, once the deed was committed, he seemed to have no particular plan, except to get out of the house and get to the Eschler's for the help he knew they'd provide. After that, he knew he was running on borrowed time.

The Capture

Gabe convinced a terrified Kelly to go with him and Jessica, but Scott wasn't having any of it. On the morning of February 22, Scott left for work. Kelly called her brother while Gabe told Jessica to start packing up the Eschler's car, because they were leaving. Kelly's brother brought over his Ford Explorer and Gabe packed up Kelly's belongings without her help or permission and began loading them into it, along with a shotgun that was kept mounted on the wall.

But the police had a surveillance team at the house and as soon as they determined that it was the Eschler car parked out front, a SWAT team was called in and the neighborhood sealed off.

Afraid for her daughter-in-law, Scott Snyder's mother called Kelly's cell phone and knowing that Gabe was probably listening, told Kelly that her mother was in the hospital and she needed Kelly to meet her there right away. Kelly knew that she was trying to tell Kelly to get out of the house, and Kelly got the message, but getting away from Gabe wasn't that easy.

An extremely agitated Gabe recognized the police surveillance and got the show on the road. Later, he said that he thought it would be better to be apprehended in a public place during a traffic stop than to have police storm the house.

When they were stopped by the police, Jessica was driving the Eschler's silver Ford Taurus with Kalea. Gabe and Kelly were in her brother's car with a shotgun in the back. They surrendered without incident. Gabe had Scott Snyder's wallet.

In a long, rambling videotaped interview, Gabriel Morris confessed to the murders, describing in detail how he ambushed his mother and Bob Kennelly, shooting from the balcony, and firing the fatal shots as he stood over them. He never said precisely why his mother had to die (rage can be like that), although he said that Kennelly had to die first because he was poisoning his family, and nothing was more important to Gabe than his family. He'd do anything for them. Secondly, he had evidence that Kennelly was thinking about sexually abusing Kalea, and nobody had ever loved a child as much as Gabe loved Kalea.

He told the story about being dropped into the ocean at age four and God granting him the power to breathe under water. He denied robbing anyone to fund their cross-country adventure.

He related with some pleasure how he intimidated his wife. "Jessica does what I tell her to do, 'cause I'm intimidating. If you've got a guy who just shot two people and he's telling you to get into a car, you're gonna get in the car. That type of woman is gonna get into the car, especially if she's got a four-year-old girl."

He fought extradition to Oregon.

Eventually, in a deal made with the Coos County District Attorney, the death penalty was removed from consideration in exchange for Morris's cooperation and stipulation to the facts that he killed Robin Anstey and Robert Kennelly Jr. He finally waived extradition and was brought back to Oregon where

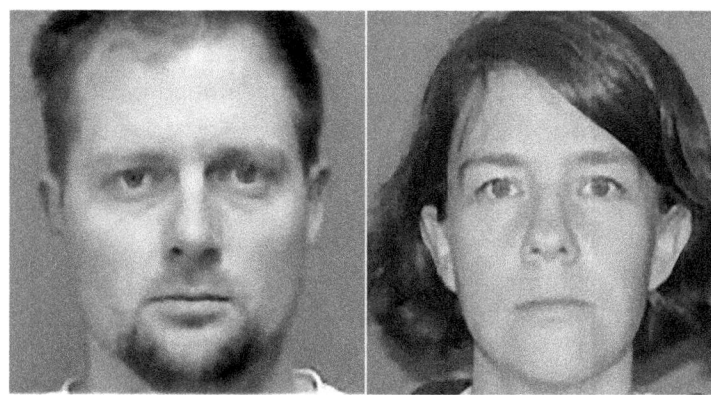

Gabriel Morris and jessica Morris
Mug Shots

he was arraigned May 6, 2010 on two counts of aggravated murder.

His defense? Insanity.

Gabriel argued with his attorney about this defense strategy, insisting that he had no mental defect, and was perfectly sane.

Jessica Morris did not fight extradition. She was brought back to Oregon and pled guilty to hindering prosecution while her parents kept Kalea. She agreed to testify against her husband and was sentenced to three years probation and fined $1344. She currently lives in Oregon with her two daughters.

The Trial

District Attorney R. Paul Frasier had his hands full. For a small county in southern Oregon with limited resources, there seemed to be a lot of murder cases to try.

Frasier left his post as Special Prosecutor at the South Coast Interagency Narcotics Team and Deputy District Attorney in Josephine County, Oregon, when Governor Ted Kulongoski asked him to take over the Coos County position from retiring DA Paul Burgett. Frasier was sworn in December 31, 2007. He inherited a serious budget problem with the loss of millions of dollars to the county's general fund as a result of the reduction of federal timber money. In an interview in January 2011, Frasier said that because of the low pay offered his new Deputy District Attorneys in Coos County, his office serves as a training position until they can find a better paying job elsewhere.

But just because the prosecutor's office has budgetary problems doesn't mean that crime stops in the small coastal community. By April 13, 2011, a Register-Guard article stated that "not yet four months into the year, [Coos] County already has topped the three killings recorded in all of 2010 and has tied the number (four) set in 2009."

Considering his budget, Frasier felt it prudent to take the death penalty off the table in return for Morris's stipulation to the fact that he committed the killings. That way, Frasier didn't

District Attorney R. Paul Frasier

have to foot the bill to retrieve witnesses from Virginia for the trial which could have lasted two weeks. Morris also waived his right to a jury trial which further streamlined things.

Along with his court-appointed defense attorneys Peter Fahy and Michael Barker, Gabriel Christian Morris faced District Attorney Paul Frasier, in Coos County Circuit Court Judge Martin Stone's courtroom for his trial which began August 9, 2011.

Judge Stone runs an efficient courtroom. A thin man with sharp dark eyes and a smooth low voice reminiscent of actor George Takei, he conducted himself with cool concern for the process. He wasted no time and kept everyone on task.

Equally on task were prosecutor Frasier and defense attorney Fahy. All three men were at ease and comfortable in their roles and they treated the defendant and every witness with respect.

The first day of testimony was dedicated to establishing the known facts of the homicides (when District Attorney Frasier referred to them as murders, defense attorney Fahy objected). Detective Sergeant Daniel Looney of the Coos County Sheriff's office testified to all of the crime scene details, and described evidence shown in many photographs displayed on a projection screen. Then Christine Karcher, a forensic nurse with the Medical Examiner's office and a member of the Major Crime Team explained the autopsy photos and charts of wounds on the bodies of the deceased. As she took the stand, defense attorney Fahy turned to family members in the gallery and wisely advised them to leave the courtroom. They stayed and listened, but the emotional nature of this particular evidence began to take its toll. Both Jesse McCoy and his uncle, Scott Walsh (Robin Anstey's brother) sat with their faces in their hands as the grisly details were described. The defendant, his reddish hair and beard about the same scruffy length, looked on with no apparent reaction.

Before the prosecution rested, they showed the hour-long video confession of the defendant, a rambling affair during

Judge Martin Stone

Coos County Court House
Oregon Secretary of State Website

which he related the story of being dropped into the ocean at four years old, said he felt that he just wants everyone to get along, and had been looking for a place where people are nice. "My plan is to love everybody," he said. When asked what he thought would have happened had a police officer walked into the house when he was confronting Kennelly about the rat poison and his plans to sexually molest Kalea, the defendant replied, "If a cop walked in, *he'd* have shot them." At the end of the interview, the defendant praised the professionalism of the SWAT team that took him and his wife safely into custody.

At the end of the first day, the prosecution read into the record some facts about the case that had already been agreed to between the parties, and then the prosecution rested.

On the second day of the trial, the defense began to call friends and family members of the defendant to the stand. The purpose was to identify Gabriel as a good-hearted human being, a devout family man who adored his mother and then had some sort of a stress-induced "crack" that altered his behavior. Again, emotions ran high when Lynn Walsh, Gabe's maternal grandmother, testified. Gabe, sitting at the defense table, asked for paper and began drawing little boxes on a legal pad, occasionally wiping his eyes. At the end of the prosecution's cross examination, she looked fondly at her grandson and said, "I will never believe that my grandson killed my daughter. Never."

In addition to the church friends of Morris, former employers and family members who testified to a similar downward trajectory in his mental state, Gabe's brother, an emotional Jesse McCoy, testified about their childhood. As he recounted some good times and some not so good times, the defendant went back to drawing little boxes on his pad, occasionally wiping his eyes with a tissue. McCoy talked about the strong bond he and his brother shared and how he always worried about him. Gabriel was only eight when Danny Morris filed for custody and won. "I had anxiety about Gabriel being okay," McCoy said.

Bullet Hole in Leaf
Police Evidence Photo

During the brothers' last phone conversation before the killings, Gabe rambled about God, his distrust of Kennelly, and his feelings of being abandoned by his mother. In this wordy monologue, Morris talked about being able to run through a forest with a blindfold on and not tripping or stumbling. He had super powers from God and was now a prophet. Had the ability to heal. Could see the future. And still could not believe that his mother had left him with Danny. But while he said he didn't like Bob Kennelly, he never said anything about his mother's safety or that he thought Bob would molest Kalea. Never, McCoy testified, did he think Robin or Bob were in any danger.

Nobody did. Nobody who testified thought Gabriel's apparent altered mental state was alarming enough to call the authorities or to think he could be a danger to himself or others.

Before the end of the day, Deputy Richard Gill testified to Morris's physical fitness. He is a model prisoner, the deputy said. He is on no medication, has had no counseling, but is busy helping others. He has taken under his wing a scared 18-year-old inmate who speaks little English, and Gabe is helping him. There is no outward evidence of mental instability.

"This case is just weird," said District Attorney Frasier in a newspaper interview after Wednesday's testimony.

The third day of testimony opened with Coquille School Board member Fred Eschler, the man to whom Gabe ran after the murders. Fred said that Gabe was good with words, tells a good story. He had a way of putting people at ease. In Fred's estimation, when Gabe and his shoeless family showed up at his doorstep on the night of February 8 with an outrageous story, he was not delusional, but in control of the situation. Fred had no reason not to believe him, so he and his wife outfitted the young family with a gun, ammunition, food, money, clothing and a car, ostensibly to get to the Air Force Base where they'd find safety. He said that if he had it to do all over again, he would act exactly as he had that night, though he had taken a lot of flak from his friends and religious community for his part in the getaway.

Continuing the third day testimony, "Big John" Lindegren testified of going out to the Kennelly place ten to twelve days before the shooting to bid a drywall job. While there, he said that Gabe was agitated, "bouncing on his heels," and that he and Kennelly weren't speaking. The prosecuting attorney, referring to an interview that Lindegren gave earlier, asked Lindegren if Gabe had met with him in his office subsequent to that appointment at the Kennelly place, and Lindegren said that he seemed like the same old Gabe. In the interview, Lindegren said Gabe had asked about acquiring a gun. On the stand, Lindegren denied having said this. Lindegren did say in response to a question that if he had to think of who might have shot Robin Anstey, that Gabe would never have even made the list.

At the end of the day, the defense attorneys announced that Morris would not testify in his own defense.

Friday, Dr. Loren Mallory testified that in his opinion, Morris suffered from a delusional disorder, marked by grandiose and religious themes. In his psychological evaluation, he notes that Morris is of above average intelligence. He "tends to present himself in a consistently favorable light, and as being relatively free of common shortcomings to which most individuals will admit. He appears reluctant to acknowledge personal limitations and will tend to repress or deny distress or other internal consequences that might arise from such limitations." The report goes on to say "This person gives evidence of limited capacity to form close attachments to other people. Although he may not necessarily avoid interpersonal relationships, these relationships tend to be psychologically at arms' length rather than up close... He shows less interest in other people than ordinarily would be expected."

Dr. Mallory suggested on the stand that things got progressively worse in the months before he shot his mother and her boyfriend, as Morris lost touch with reality. The District Attorney challenged that diagnosis, and asked if he could be certain that Morris was not lying about his delusions. He offered another motive, the $25,000 that the defendant owed Kennelly for the marijuana business. Dr. Mallory responded, "Yeah, if you want to say that he would kill him for owing him $25,000, you could say that."

People have been killed for far less.

The only witness called to the stand on Tuesday was Laura Eschler, who, along with her husband, gave Gabe and his family provisions to leave the state after the murders. She testified that he seemed himself, seemed in control that night.

In closing arguments, defense attorney Peter Fahy claimed that Morris acted on his paranoid delusions that Kennelly was trying to poison his family, that God was talking to him and that he was a prophet, perhaps even Jesus Christ himself. He self-medicated with marijuana and alcohol, confusing things further, but used the substances to try to quell the chaos in his mind. Fahy went through a list of things that a rational person would not do, such as standing on the balcony to open fire when a trained police officer such as Morris would find a better position from which to make his ambush. Then Morris left the scene without even retrieving his identification or putting on a pair of shoes.

Frasier argued that Morris' actions before, during, and after the killings weren't those of an insane person. Morris had a long history of making up elaborate lies and then bragging about how he got away with them. Frasier said that Morris was in control of himself and that he knew what he was doing was a crime. The way he drove up the driveway, parking so that Anstey and Kennelly would not see the truck. He shot Anstey four times and Kennelly five, making certain they were dead before he left. "The defendant knew he shot those people, and that what he did was against the law," Frasier said. He stole money and gift cards from the dead man and cooked up a story for the Eschlers. "That was just a story I told so I could get a car and get out of there," Morris told Virginia authorities. He threw away the murder weapon and later bragged to police that they'd never find it. These were all the calculated choices of someone who knew he had committed a crime and was trying to get away with it, Frasier said.

Morris may have some mental defect, Frasier argued, but an insanity defense requires not just a mental defect, but one that prevents the person from having the capacity to appreciate his criminal conduct.

In Oregon, in order to find someone not guilty by reason of insanity, the person must "lack substantial capacity either to appreciate the criminality of the conduct or to conform the conduct to the requirements of law." Even if Morris is found to have a mental defect, or a personality disorder, this does not constitute insanity if he was aware that what he was doing was wrong or had the capacity to control his conduct. According to court documents, "This is an affirmative defense, requiring the defendant to prove the defense by a preponderance of the evidence."

Disturbing behavior does not constitute insanity.

Mental disease is not something on which a blood test which can be performed and upon which an absolute diagnosis can be made. In making a mental health diagnosis, again according to court documents, the medical practitioner must rely upon the symptoms and actions of the person in order to make the diagnosis. If the person is not telling the truth to the doctor, the validity of the diagnosis is in question.

In the plaintiff's trial memorandum, Frasier writes: The defendant's credibility is almost non-existent. He will lie at any opportunity. He lied about why he left Air Force ROTC. He lied about being in the Air Force and being part of a special operations team. He lied about why he left the sheriff's office in Idaho. He lied to Allie Smith about getting a divorce from Jessica. He cheated Allie Smith by improperly using her credit cards. He lied to Jessica when he denied being sexually involved with Allie Smith and Kelly Love. He lied to Bill Pope about what opportunities he had with James Anstey in order to get Bill Pope to loan him money and a truck. He lied to the

Eschlers about what happened.

He lies when it is in his best interest to do so. Clearly, he's capable of lying to a psychologist.

After a two-hour lunch break, Judge Stone pronounced his verdict: guilty on two counts of aggravated murder. "He was in control when he moved down to the ground level and finished off the victims by shooting them as they lay dying on the ground," Judge Stone said. "Mr. Morris is not a dummy. He's intelligent, articulate, he has training as a police officer. His actions speak volumes. Those actions are not the actions of a person who is delusional."

Before sentencing, Morris addressed the court. "There's a million things I could say, but I'm not necessarily sure this is the best environment to say them in," he said. "I'm proud of my family and friends, not for what they said about me, but I'm grateful for their love and support…I pray we live in a society that can heal and change things the way they are."

Judge Stone then delivered his sentence: two consecutive life terms in prison without the possibility of parole.

Conclusion

The question remains: Why did Gabe Morris kill his mother? This is a question that not even he seems able to answer. All we have is his cryptic answer to his wife when she asked him why he did it: "Because it had to be done."

Two scenarios are likely.

The first is that he went back to the house that day fully intending to confront Bob about his share of the living expenses, the $25,000 loan, the marijuana business and a few other things. But while he waited those long eight hours, he chewed on all manner of injustices, beginning with his perception that his mother abandoned him to the hands of his abusive father when he was a child. He ran scenarios in his head, he ran dialogues ("If he says this, then I'll say that") until his rage became so overwhelming that by the time they

Robin Anstey
Family Photo

returned home, he could have talked himself into believing just about anything, but most of all, he believed that "It had to be done."

In "The Role of Psychopathology and Personality in Rage-Type Homicide," author Duncan Cartwright notes that "An act of murder driven primarily by an uncontrollable explosive rage reaction has been found by many to be a common form of homicidal behavior. What makes establishing a psychological profile of these kinds of offenders particularly intriguing is that most are classified as apparently 'normal' individuals. 'Normal' is used here to refer to offenders who do not typically have a history of violence or enduring psychopathology." The author goes on to note that long parental absences and a chaotic family background usually characterized emotional deprivation.

Another scenario is that Morris began planning this day a long time ago, perhaps in his childhood fantasies. No matter what he did as an adult, he couldn't get the type of attention he wanted from his mother, the primal source of a deflated ego and lifetime of humiliating events. He authored those events but wasn't strong enough emotionally to be able to triumph over them as would a person with a healthy ego. Gabe worked at the Idaho State Mental Hospital, and perhaps he did some research by observing how crazy people act and took the time to perfect his manic persona so that people actually believed that he had suffered a breakdown. He seemed to systematically try this role on with people who knew him as humble Gabriel Morris, but he wasn't altogether consistent with this act, at least not consistent enough to get away with murder.

In "The Narcissistic Exoskeleton: The Defensive Organization of the Rage-Type Murderer," author Duncan Cartwright argues that for those with Borderline Personality Disorder, the "bad self" remains concealed behind the narcissistic exoskeleton. As a result, bad experience simply accumulates and remains unmodified and unarticulated. The separation between the external fantasy and internal reality as representation of idealized good objects and all-bad objects is important to maintain. Persons in this category are prone to violence that is catastrophically violent or homicidal. The coherent ego is maintained as long as the destructive and disturbed area of the personality remains split off.

The author continues that "Hate and consequential fear are key factors that create an oversensitivity in violent individuals. In a transient form, this is not an uncommon experience for most of us. Prolonged hate, however, causes even greater sensitivity, and murder itself is seen as a fantasized end to these distressing emotions." Also, the author contends, "[this type of murderer] possesses a particular habitual kind of magical thinking that is supremely arrogant. Underneath this arrogance, however, these individuals often feel inferior and incompetent and are extremely passive. Violence or murder frees them from these disabling factors in the personality." Continuing, he states, "These individuals internalize a strong need to depend on the maternal object, conform, and succeed. However, due to their insecurities and confusion regarding their own identity and underlying hostility, they constantly fail. This tension sets up a cycle of personal failures that leads to escalating feelings of anger and rage. And then, the violent act is carried out followed by a superficial return to normality, *but with no insight into the event.*"

In discussing rage murders in those diagnosed with Borderline Personality Disorder, Cartwright says that offenders have poor impulse control, transient blurring of fantasy and reality, altered states of consciousness, shallow or blunted affect, and finally a violent and primitive fantasy life.

In the end, perhaps "it had to be done" in order for Morris to free himself from the guilt of not being able to protect his mother as well as never living up to his own expectations of himself in every other area. There was a way out. There was a way out of all that responsibility of being a husband and a father and a son-in-law and a son and a brother. There was a way out of financial obligations and trying to make a living. There was a way out of all the hassles and pressures of life and family amid myriad temptations. There was a solution whereby he could just focus on that which he always really wanted to do: help others. Perhaps he envisioned himself in a hospital for ten years or so helping others.

That part of his fantasy didn't exactly happen according to plan. Instead, he shattered the lives of all who knew and loved him. Mental defect or no, we all have a million tiny choices every single day. Gabriel Morris made all the wrong choices.

Bibliography

Bandon Western World. "Robert William Bob Kennelly, Jr." 25 February 2010

Boudreau, Damian "Frasier takes over as district attorney". *The World* [Bandon] 4 January 2008

Carmack, Laurie. Email to the author. 2 September 2011

Cartwright, Duncan. "The narcissistic exoskeleton: the defensive organization of the rage-type murderer." *Bulletin Of The Menninger Clinic* 66.1 (2002): 1-18. *MEDLINE with Full Text*. EBSCO. Web. 9 Sept. 2011.

Cartwright, Duncan. "The role of psychopathology and personality in rage-type homicide: a review." *South African Journal of Psychology* 31.3 (2001): 12. *Academic Search Complete*. EBSCO. Web. 9 Sept. 2011.

Heide, Kathleen M. "Why kids kill parents." *Psychology Today* 25.5 (1992): 62. *MasterFILE Premier*. EBSCO. Web. 9 Sept. 2011.

Olsen, Hannah, "Psychologist Takes Stand in Gabriel Morris Trial" Ross, Winston. "Morris Gets Life Sentence" *The Register-Guard* [Eugene] 17 August 2011.

— "Murder Suspect Returned to Oregon" *The Register-Guard* [Eugene] 6 May 2010: B1

— "Promise and Tragedy" *The Register-Guard* [Eugene] 14 March 2010: A1

— "Suspect arrested in Bandon couple's slaying" *The Register-Guard* [Eugene] 23 February 2010: A1

—"Homicides shake up Coos County" *The Register-Guard* [Eugene] 13 April 2011: B1

Walsh, Scott. Personal interview. 25 August, 2011

About the Author

Elizabeth Engstrom is the author of seventeen books and many short stories, articles and essays. She is a sought-after speaker and instructor at conferences and conventions around the world.

Engstrom's interest in crime writing is not new; her critically-acclaimed 1990 novel about axe-murderer Lizzie Borden remains a research tool for the never-ending speculation on that unsolved case.

www.ElizabethEngstrom.com

IFD Publishing Paperbacks

Novels:
Of Thimble and Threat, by Alan M. Clark
Baggage Check, by Elizabeth Engstrom
Bull's Labyrinth, by Eric Witchey
The Surgeon's Mate: A Dismemoir, by Alan M. Clark
Siren Promised, by Jeremy Robert Johnson and Alan M. Clark
Say Anything but Your Prayers, by Alan M. Clark
Candyland, by Elizabeth Engstrom
Apologies to the Cat's Meat Man, by Alan M. Clark
Lizzie Borden, by Elizabeth Engstrom
A Parliament of Crows, by Alan M. Clark
Lizard Wine, by Elizabeth Engstrom
The Door that Faced West, by Alan M. Clark
The Northwoods Chronicles, by Elizabeth Engstrom
The Prostitute's Price, by Alan M. Clark
The Assassin's Coin, by John Linwood Grant
13 Miller's Court, by Alan M. Clark and John Linwood Grant
Guys Named Bob, by Elizabeth Engstrom

Collections:
Professor Witchey's Miracle Mood Cure, by Eric Witchey

Nonfiction:
How to Write a Sizzling Sex Scene, by Elizabeth Engstrom

IFD Publishing EBooks

(You can find the following titles at most distribution points for all ereading platforms.)

Novels:
The Prostitute's Price, by Alan M. Clark
The Assassin's Coin, by John Linwood Grant
13 Miller's Court, by Alan M. Clark and John Linwood Grant
Guys Named Bob, by Elizabeth Engstrom
Apologies to the Cat's Meat Man, by Alan M. Clark
Bull's Labyrinth, by Eric Witchey

The Surgeon's Mate: A Dismemoir, by Alan M. Clark
York's Moon, by Elizabeth Engstrom
Beyond the Serpent's Heart, by Eric Witchey
Lizzie Borden, by Elizabeth Engstrom
A Parliament of Crows, by Alan M. Clark
Lizard Wine, by Elizabeth Engstrom
Northwoods Chronicles, by Elizabeth Engstrom
Siren Promised, by Alan M. Clark and Jeremy Robert Johnson
To Kill a Common Loon, by Mitch Luckett
The Man in the Loon, by Mitch Luckett
Jack the Ripper Victim Series: Of Thimble and Threat by Alan M. Clark
Jack the Ripper Victim Series: The Double Event (includes two novels from the series: *Of Thimble and Threat* and *Say Anything But Your Prayers*) by Alan M. Clark
Candyland, by Elizabeth Engstrom
The Blood of Father Time: Book 1, The New Cut, by Alan M. Clark, Stephen C. Merritt & Lorelei Shannon
The Blood of Father Time: Book 2, The Mystic Clan's Grand Plot, by Alan M. Clark, Stephen C. Merritt & Lorelei Shannon
How I Met My Alien Bitch Lover: Book 1 from the Sunny World Inquisition Daily Letter Archives, by Eric Witchey
Baggage Check, by Elizabeth Engstrom
D. D. Murphry, Secret Policeman, by Alan M. Clark and Elizabeth Massie
Black Leather, by Elizabeth Engstrom

Novelettes:
The Tao of Flynn, by Eric Witchey
To Build a Boat, Listen to Trees, by Eric Witchey

Children's Illustrated:
The Christmas Thingy, by F. Paul Wilson. Illustrated by Alan M. Clark

Collections:
Suspicions, by Elizabeth Engstrom

Professor Witchey's Miracle Mood Cure, by Eric Witchey

Short Fiction:
"Brittle Bones and Old Rope," by Alan M. Clark
"Crosley," by Elizabeth Engstrom
"The Apple Sniper," by Eric Witchey

Nonfiction:
How to Write a Sizzling Sex Scene, by Elizabeth Engstrom
Divorce by Grand Canyon, by Elizabeth Engstrom

IFD Publishing Audio Books

Novels:

The Door That Faced West by Alan M. Clark, read by Charles Hinckley

Jack the Ripper Victim Series: Of Thimble and Threat, by Alan M. Clark, read by Alicia Rose

Jack the Ripper Victim Series: Say Anything But Your Prayers, by Alan M. Clark, read by Alicia Rose

Jack the Ripper Victim Series: The Double Event by Alan M. Clark, read by Alicia Rose (includes two novels from the series: *Of Thimble and Threat* and *Say Anything But Your Prayers*)

A Parliament of Crows by Alan M. Clark, read by Laura Jennings

A Brutal Chill in August by Alan M. Clark, read by Alicia Rose

The Surgeon's Mate: A Dismemoir, by Alan M. Clark, read by Alan M. Clark

Apologies to the Cat's Meat Man, by Alan M. Clark, read by Alicia Rose

The Prostitute's Price, by Alan M. Clark, read by Alicia Rose

The Assassin's Coin, by John Linwood Grant, read by Alicia Rose

13 Miller's Court, by Alan M. Clark and John Linwood Grant, read by Alicia Rose

www.ingramcontent.com/pod-product-compliance
Lightning Source LLC
Chambersburg PA
CBHW061649040426
42446CB00010B/1651